MARXIST PHILOSOPHY

MARXIST PHILOSOPHY

A BIBLIOGRAPHICAL GUIDE

by JOHN LACHS

THE UNIVERSITY OF
NORTH CAROLINA PRESS
CHAPEL HILL

Copyright © 1967 by
The University of North Carolina Press
Manufactured in the United States of America
Printed by Heritage Printers, Inc., Charlotte, N. C.
Library of Congress Catalog Card Number 67–27158

For

MARGARET AND HUTTY TITMUS

CONTENTS

INTRODUCTION

A bibliography has only one conceivable justification: its usefulness. Even the prospect of producing something useful, however, would never have occasioned me to compile a bibliography of the philosophy of Marxism. My main interest is in the substance of philosophical problems; I gladly leave the collection of references and the sorting of cards to those whose native bent and special training enable them to excel at these activities.

When I began my study of the philosophical foundations of Marxism-Leninism, I hoped to find some book that would quickly guide me to the major expository and critical works on each of the topics I wished to examine. Within a short time it became painfully clear that no such book existed. The few bibliographies that were available proved to be woefully inadequate, either because their coverage was too narrow or because they contained too many biased judgments about the philosophical value of the books they reviewed. Without a map or compass I was cast upon the waves of those books and pamphlets that flood the darker corners of libraries.

This bibliographical guide is a by-product of my attempt to chart a course through these stormy depths (and too often, I am afraid, shallows). What led to its publication was not the languid hope of producing something useful but the recognition of an urgent need. If the information I have collected will help some scholar, student, or interested layman to obtain the literature he needs without confusing hours in the stacks, my long weeks with *The Journal of Philosophy* and with more issues of *The Labour Monthly* than I care to recall will not have been spent in vain.

This is a bibliographical guide to the philosophy of Marxism. The phrase "Marxist philosophy" is here taken in a wide sense. It is taken as the name of the group of theories that is usually thought to constitute the world view of dialectical and historical materialism. This group contains theories about the nature and constituents of the universe, the structure and development of societies, the fulfillment of the individual, and the methods of obtaining knowledge, among others. For the sake of clarity I have attempted to distinguish and give a separate section to as many of these theories as seemed feasible. In order to promote philosophical perspective and the creative controversy that often leads to new insight or better understanding, I have included critical as well as expository works in almost every section. I am certain that no cause would have been served by my taking the usual distinction between Marxism and Marxism-Leninism so seriously as to exclude important works of one or the other. Instead, I have tried to make relevance to the philosophical issues comprised under the general heading of dialectical and historical materialism the major (though not the sole) criterion of inclusion.

This is, on the whole, a bibliographical guide to philosophical works. Admittedly, in dealing with a philosophy that insists on the unity of thought and action, it is only by a decision, at least in part arbitrary, that we may draw the line between what is relevant to theory and what is of purely practical concern. I do not agree with Rudas' absurd suggestion that to understand the revolutionary theories of dialectical materialism one must "sooner or later" enroll in the ranks of the revolutionary party.[1] But there is little doubt that an examination of certain practical issues, actions, and debates in the history of the Communist movement tends to throw an unusual amount of light on the philosophical theories that undergird them. For this reason, I have chosen to include a good deal that is not, in the usual view, of immediate philosophical interest, among them some books on Soviet educational practice and the better part of a section on the genetics controversy that centered around the figure and theories of Lysenko. I have, however, resolutely avoided the inclusion of any titles that do not go beyond consideration of the practical issues of the moment.

If it is not easy to draw the line between theory and practice in Marxism or Marxism-Leninism, it is doubly difficult to mark off

[1] Ladislaus Rudas, "Dialectical Materialism and Communism," *The Labour Monthly* 15 (1933), 569.

their sociological from their philosophical, their economic from their political, and their historical from their metaphysical theories. Acting on the assumption that it is not necessary to have specialized training in economics for an understanding of the philosophy of Marx and his followers, I have excluded all books and articles whose main emphasis is on technical economics. However, I have listed a number of titles in the fields of sociology, psychology, and political science. The items relating to political economy, psychiatry, and the theory of law have been included because of the insight they afford into more properly philosophical topics.

The principle that governed the selection and organization of the entries has been that of practical use. Accordingly, on the assumption that few scholars are fluent in more than three languages, I have limited my materials to what is available in English, French, and German. I have, of course, not attempted to attain completeness: knowledge of everything ever printed about dialectical and historical materialism in three languages must always remain, I am quite certain, a minor but exclusive achievement of Omniscience. Since all-inclusiveness, even if it were possible, would serve no purpose, I have unhesitatingly omitted many titles that, in my opinion, did not contribute to an understanding of the topic they set out to discuss. I have eliminated a large number of propaganda pamphlets, as well as most, though not all, books that showed crippling philosophical incompetence. I have not listed a number of works that are of marginal value or are extremely difficult to get. I have also left out titles that have (in some cases for good reason) long been out of print.

I have made certain that my list of books in English—clearly of the greatest potential value to English-speaking scholars—is the least incomplete. The German and French lists are less inclusive due partly to the fact that whenever an English translation of a work was available, I have listed it only in English and partly to the practical consideration that substantially fewer French and German language than English language books are available in United States and British libraries. It is important to call attention to this last limitation: my French and German selections are particularly geared to the holdings of United States libraries at the time of this writing. East German houses have launched ambitious programs of translation and publication in the last decade; very few of the resulting books, however, are generally available in this country. Throughout the bibliography, my aim has been to provide not only most of the central works on every topic treated, but also a total number of references somewhat in excess of what one is likely to find in a good university library, and substantially in excess of what one is likely to need for ordinary research purposes. The person particularly interested in current German work or in German translations from the Russian may refer to the catalogues of such East German publishers as Dietz Verlag and Deutscher Verlag der Wissenschaften. To keep abreast of the literature in English, the reader should not neglect to consult from time to time the growing list of books released by Foreign Languages Publishing House, Moscow.

Although I have listed a considerable number of journal articles, the emphasis of the bibliography is on books. Some journals, such as *Science and Society*, publish articles on dialectical materialism and related subjects only; others, such as *Survey*, follow the Soviet cultural and philosophical scene. Virtually every issue of such journals and magazines contains a number of relevant articles. To avoid the expansion of this bibliographical guide to unmanageable size which would result from listing each of their articles as a separate entry, I have devoted a section to listing the journals themselves. The introductory remarks in that section (Section 37) should help the reader to decide which, if any, of the seventy-seven journals included can be expected to yield further information on his topic of interest. For the sake of reasonable brevity, I have, of course, also avoided listing book reviews.

I have devoted a special section to the "classics" of Marxism-Leninism and another to relevant bibliographies. The limitation of the "classics" to Marx, Engels, Lenin, Stalin, and Mao is somewhat arbitrary, though not indefensible. The selection, however, is not meant to prejudice any issues: the function of the section is simply to call the reader's attention to some of the oft-quoted central statements of historical and dialectical materialism. This section had best be consulted first in one's research; it is unlikely, however, that the bibliographical section will be of much use before one's reading and reflection are well advanced. I have chosen to include but a few discussions of dialectical and historical materialism in encyclopedias and histories of philosophy. An important part of the reason for this is the unavoidable superficiality of all such treatments. The few I have listed might be used as helpful introductory readings of a general sort, but it is important to remember that there is nothing about Marxist philosophy in histories of philosophy or in encyclopedias that is not said with equal conciseness and greater precision in works devoted to that subject alone.

The person especially interested in the relation of Marx, Engels, and Lenin to major figures in the history of philosophy will find a number of interesting items listed. However, I have not thought it necessary to list any of the works of those who are considered precursors of Marx. I have also neglected to give space to those who might have benefited in some way from Marx's thought without, however, writing about Marx or becoming Marxists. The person who wishes to study Soviet Marxism-Leninism will find an ample list of references. The specialist in this field, however, will receive little help, mainly because I have cited no Soviet sources other than those that are available in translation.

I have chosen the simplest form of reference adequate to carry the information I wished to convey. Whenever possible, I selected a good and available edition of the work I wished to include. To keep my entries to a reasonable number, I have refrained from listing multiple editions and paperback reprints. I have introduced the names of translators only where this seemed important or appropriate. In each section, English, French, and German titles are listed separately, in that order. Within each language, a list of books is followed by a list of articles; the two lists are separately alphabetized. For ease of reference each entry is numbered. The list of numbers at the end of each section refers to the works that contain important but subsidiary discussions of the section's topic. The bibliography contains no works published after December 31, 1966.

I wish to express my gratitude to the late Mr. E. Hutson Titmus, Jr., without whose encouragement and generous support this bibliography could not have been prepared. Miss Margaret C. Weirick's assistance was invaluable throughout the project; in addition to her able help with the research, she also typed and proofread the manuscript. I also wish to thank Professors Thomas J. Blakeley, I. M. Bocheński, David D. Comey, Richard T. DeGeorge, Donald C.

Hodges, George L. Kline, Herbert Marcuse, Howard L. Parsons, John Somerville, and Robert C. Tucker for giving me much-needed leads with the bibliography. My special thanks go to Professor Frank A. MacDonald for being a good friend and a helpful colleague and to the College of William and Mary for the readiness with which it has assisted me throughout the course of this project.

MARXIST PHILOSOPHY

I ──────── THE LITERATURE
OF MARXIST PHILOSOPHY

It is probable that in the past hundred years there have been more books and articles published on the vaguely circumscribed topic of "Communism" than on any other, with the exception of Christianity. A considerable portion of this flood of literature deals at least in part with dialectical materialism, historical materialism, or some related issue. One would expect—especially if one took the laws of the dialectic seriously—that quantity of this magnitude would have produced high quality. Unfortunately, however, this is not the case, and on the whole dialectical and historical materialism remains among those major philosophical theories that have received the least adequate conceptual elaboration and the hastiest evaluation.

There are many reasons for this failure of serious study. One of them is graphically demonstrated by the proliferation of introductory booklets. Although many of these "introductions to dialectical materialism" contain some philosophical material, their main purpose is not to further inquiry but to convince the untutored reader. Communists sometimes justify this propagandistic use of philosophical ideas by claiming that the theories of historical and dialectical materialism are, perhaps first and foremost, a revolutionary weapon. Anti-communists sometimes justify their facile refutations of Marxist philosophy by maintaining that fire has to be fought with fire. Unfortunately, such Marxist-Leninist popularizers appear to forget that it is at best a tenet of their theory that philosophies are primarily weapons in the class war. To justify this tenet, their theories have to be investigated thoroughly and in depth. The opponents of Marxism-Leninism, on the other hand, are forgetful of their oft-quoted allegiance to truth, wherever it may lead; in their impromptu refutations of the Marxist they have adopted his view that propaganda comes first and abandoned the conviction that the unhurried glimpse of truth in the end always prevails.

A second reason for the dearth of substantial philosophical investigation in the field of Marxist philosophy grows directly out of the first. Since the purpose of a good deal of writing on the subject is persuasion, not inquiry, the exchanges between exponents of conflicting views tend to be diatribes rather than dialogues. Confronted with some objection to their views, Marxists frequently resort to one of three techniques to counter it. The first is a simple form of the *argumentum ad hominem*; the attempt is made to refute the critic's ideas by reviling his character, impugning his motives, or defining him out of significant human existence as a "revisionist," "opportunist," or "capitalist lackey." The second technique is known in textbooks of logic as the *ignoratio elenchi* fallacy. It consists of finding a view that is patently absurd but bears a certain superficial similarity to the critic's actual position. The absurd view is first attributed to the critic and then thoroughly exposed, ridiculed, and refuted. In this way the Marxist may eliminate the objection without ever having to assess its actual force. Even as acute a thinker as Lenin did not hesitate to use these two methods to dispose of philosophical antagonists. The third technique frequently employed by the Marxist in defense of his beliefs is that of finding suitable quotes in the works of Marx, Engels, or Lenin to establish that the critic's view is not theirs, and therefore not true. This method has a certain similarity to the techniques of justification used by theologians in quoting the Scriptures (a similarity that did not escape the attention of anti-communist critics), but it bears no resemblance to rational philosophical method.

Many of the opponents of dialectical and historical materialism are, I am afraid, equally guilty of bad practices in argumentation. At the one extreme there are those who need no more than a comparison of the texts of Marx with those of St. Thomas Aquinas to determine the truth about Marxist philosophy. Not all prejudices are, of course, so disarmingly unsubtle. Too many critics of Marxism-Leninism have approached its philosophical views with a commitment to theism, some partisan view of human nature or liberal democracy which, though tacit, was powerful enough to cripple their attempts at unbiased investigation. The kind of dispassionate philosophical inquiry that is common in such fields as the theory of perception, and even ethics, is relatively infrequent in dialectical and historical materialism. Where everyone has an axe to grind, not much wood gets chopped; the heat of such controversy promotes many causes, but philosophical enlightenment is not one of them.

I shall discuss only one more contributing cause of the relative shortage of philosophically important works on dialectical and historical materialism. Whatever the reason for this may be, many Marxists are too often satisfied with purely verbal or with pictorial "sotions" to philosophical problems. Critics have, on the whole, no een quick to challenge such legerdemain. The best examples of e purely verbal solution derive perhaps from the Marxist-Leninist use of the law of the unity of opposites. A multitude of pairs, whose members stand in very different sorts of relations to one another, have all been called "opposites." I could not find a single book that presented an adequate discussion of the precise meaning of "opposites" and of "unity" in the context of this law. In the absence of clear criteria of application, these words can be employed to signify a wide variety of things, and the "law" in the formulation of which they occur may be used to give the impression of opening many an embarrassing philosophical *cûl-de-sac*.

A useful example of a picture that has the power to blind able thinkers is the frequently quoted one of the mind or of knowledge as the "reflection" of reality. This metaphor is sometimes billed as "the foundation" of Marxist-Leninist epistemology. Now I must confess I do not think it is much of a foundation for anything, much less for an entire theory of knowledge. It is no more than a metaphor: though useful for leading one's mind in a certain direction, it resolves no problems. And its vast disadvantage is that, like a light flashed in the eye instead of the dark corners of the room, it hides rather than reveals the issues that must be resolved. Despite this fact, I have been unable to find a single dialectical materialist who showed himself substantially dissatisfied with the metaphor or who made a serious attempt to work out its full consequences.

The desire for propaganda, the bent for diatribe, and the satisfaction with metaphor may help explain the philosophical weaknesses in the literature of dialectical and historical materialism, but they do not excuse it. Professor Bocheński is of the opinion that the mind-body problem in Soviet philosophy is on a level as primitive as that of the pre-Socratics.[1] Whether this is true, and whether Professor Bocheński's claim should be extended from Soviet philosophy to most dialectical materialists and from the mind-body problem to many another central philosophical issue, is not my present purpose to determine. It is, however, important to take account of the lacunae in the literature, and one of the tasks of a bibliographical guide such as this is to hasten this recognition.

It would be unfair to end on this negative note. Some excellent and a good deal of solid work has already been done on a number of topics relating to Marxist philosophy. Research on Marx's relation to his predecessors has yielded thorough and important studies. Although much remains to be done on the place of Marx and Engels in the history of philosophy, we have already learned a great deal about their relation to Hegel, Feuerbach, and such figures as Hess and Stirner as a result of work published in the last thirty-five years. There is great current interest in the young Marx, and while some valuable books have already appeared, it is reasonable to expect important further developments in the near future.

From the early 1930's there has been considerable interest in Marxist and Marxist-Leninist theories of art, literary criticism, and aesthetics. Marxist aestheticians share the weakness of most of their non-Marxist colleagues in not knowing enough epistemology, while they have the additional disadvantage of having their

---

[1] Innocentius M. Bocheński, "On Soviet Philosophy," *The Review of Politics* 13 (1951), 351.

heads full of sociological theories. Their opponents, on the other hand, share the weakness of literary critics in firmly refusing not to be blinded by their prejudices. As a result many uninformed, even silly, things have been said about the theory of socialist realism and related issues on both sides of the controversy. Luckily, however, some of the literature has escaped crippling partisan bias and managed to reach the stage of being both insightful and objective.

There are other bright spots. Even though the historical and the philosophical elements are not usually disentangled in discussions of historical materialism, several of the more important issues in this area (among them the distinction between the economic substructure and the ideological superstructure) have received incisive scrutiny. It is to be hoped that before long we shall also see thorough discussions of historical materialism in the context of the contemporary controversy over the logic of historical explanation. Some promising work has been done on the dialectical materialist philosophy of science, even though this is a field in which much more investigation is required. The philosophical implications of the Lysenko affair were, on the whole, well explored. Finally, we are fortunate to have an increasing flow of information about Soviet thought as a result of the work of the translation journal *Soviet Studies in Philosophy* and of the members of such organizations as the Institute of East-European Studies at the University of Fribourg, publisher of *Studies in Soviet Thought*. Although the works of many students of Soviet philosophy more nearly resemble reports than close philosophical analysis, their contribution deserves greater appreciation than it has so far received.

In spite of these scattered strengths in the literature, it is important to remind ourselves that dialectical and historical materialism has never enjoyed careful philosophical attention of the magnitude that has recently been lavished on the logic of explanation or of the incisiveness that has long been expended on the theory of perception. For this reason, if for no other, to say that much remains to be done on the examination of Marxist philosophy is to understate the task more than good sense will allow. It is, I believe, more nearly correct to maintain that although the "classics" of Marxist philosophy have long been available to everyone, the classic philosophical elaborations and assessments of the views of Marx, Engels, and Lenin are yet to be written.

2 ─────────────────── THE CLASSICS
OF MARXIST PHILOSOPHY

It is sound to begin one's research with the original sources.
The beginner, therefore, may well start with 8, which is the complete text of the famous early work of Marx never published in
his lifetime. The notion of alienation is of central significance at
this stage in Marx's development: many similarities to existentialism are thought to have been detected by scholars. 7 contains the
Bottomore translation of the 1844 Manuscripts, along with another
important early work entitled *Contributions to the Critique of
Hegel's Philosophy of Right*. 944 contains selections from the
Manuscripts, along with a useful but in places quite inaccurate
introduction by Erich Fromm.

2 is an edition of Volume 1 of Marx's most important work.
This is laborious reading and only isolated passages have direct
philosophical relevance. Yet it must be carefully examined by
every serious student of Marx. 1 is the full three-volume edition of
Capital in good translation. 11 is a group of selections from Marx's
preliminary manuscripts for the projected fourth volume of the
work.

In studying the original statements of historical materialism,
special attention should be paid to 5, 6, 10, 18, 20, 33, and 34. 19 is
the first translation into English of the complete text of *The German Ideology*. In 9 Marx assails the French philosopher Proudhon;
20 is a withering attack on some of Marx's German contemporaries.

Although 17 is a remarkable document, its theoretical signifi-

cance is often overestimated. It is, first and foremost, a manifesto—
a public declaration of views—without elucidation or defense. 16,
22, 23, and 28 are useful selections collating virtually all of Marx's
and Engel's important statements on topics announced in the titles.
24 contains most though not all of the essential letters; 21 adds
some others. In both books there are comments on a wide range
of philosophical issues.

There is no complete edition of the works of Marx and Engels
in any of the three languages of this bibliography. 26, though incomplete, was until recently generally considered the authoritative
edition. It is now being replaced by the excellent 27, which will,
eventually, be complete. 29 contains a number of items from the
period of 1841 to 1850, which may be of value to the advanced
researcher. It is to be hoped that someday we might have the complete Marx-Engels corpus readily available in a good English
translation; the production of this, however, would involve a
staggering amount of effort and expense. Philosophers who read no
German now have to be satisfied with such a standard small
edition as 25.

Engels' 30, 31, and 32 are of central philosophical interest. 30
contains important statements on virtually every major aspect of
dialectical and historical materialism. 31 has from the first been
perhaps the major source of the Marxist-Leninist philosophy of
nature. 32 discusses the contrast between materialism and idealism:
it is a classic text of Marxist-Leninist metaphysics.

Lenin's *Collected Works* (35) includes a great deal that is of
little philosophical significance. But it contains his important
Philosophical Notebooks, which constitute his most sophisticated
contribution to thought. 45 is a standard small edition of Lenin's
works. 40 is a major, albeit in many places confused, work in
epistemology. Lenin's contributions to the Marxist theory of capitalism are best seen in 36. 48 is a major statement on the historical
materialist theory of the nature and role of the state, the causes of
revolution, and the subsequent development of society through
the dictatorship of the proletariat to the second stage of communism. Related discussions may be found in 41, 46, 47, and 52.
38 and 43 are largely polemical in character: they are directed
against revisionism. 37, 49 and 50 are introductory.

Stalin's contributions to philosophy do not warrant a separate chapter in any history of thought, no matter how detailed. Most of his theoretical writing is of the nature of summaries; the rest relates immediately to the practical issues of the day. 55 is a successful simplification of the principles of historical and dialectical materialism. Because of its labored clarity, it is a good general introduction to the field. 54, 59, 61, and 63 have a strong practical orientation. 56 and 57 argue that Leninism is the correct further development of the work of Marx. 58 is an unconvincing statement about linguistics by one who knew not very much about it. 60 is the report of an interview between Stalin and H. G. Wells. 64 is a standard, though incomplete, collection of Stalin's works in English.

Although there may be considerable argument about giving Mao's works full acknowledgement as "classics" of Marxist philosophy, it is at least appropriate to mention him in this context. 65 includes "On Practice" and "On Contradiction," two of Mao's more properly philosophical works.

1. MARX, KARL. *Capital, A Critical Analysis of Capitalist Production.* Moscow: Foreign Languages Publishing House, 1961. 3 vols.
2. ———. *Capital; A Critique of Political Economy.* New York: The Modern Library, 1936. 869p.
3. ———. *Capital; A Critique of Political Economy.* Chicago: Kerr, 1925–26. 3 vols.
4. ———. *The Class Struggles in France (1848–1850).* New York: International Publishers, 1964. 158p.
5. ———. *A Contribution to the Critique of Political Economy.* New York: The International Library Publishing Company, 1904. 314p.
6. ———. *Critique of the Gotha Programme.* New York: International Publishers, 1938. 116p.
7. ———. *Early Writings.* London: Universal Distributors, 1963. 227p.
8. ———. *The Economic and Philosophic Manuscripts of 1844.* New York: International Publishers, 1964. 255p.
9. ———. *The Poverty of Philosophy.* New York: International Publishers, 1964. 256p.
10. ———. *Pre-Capitalist Economic Formations.* New York: International Publishers, 1965. 153p.

11. ——. *Theories of Surplus Value*. New York: International Publishers, 1952. 432p.
12. ——. *Grundrisse der Kritik der Politischen Oekonomie (Rohentwurf)*. Berlin: Dietz, 1953.
13. BLACKSTOCK, PAUL W., and HOSELITZ, BERT F., eds. *The Russian Menace to Europe*. London: Allen & Unwin, 1953. 288p.
14. BOTTOMORE, T. B., and RUBEL, MAXIMILIEN, eds. *Karl Marx: Selected Writings in Sociology and Social Philosophy*. London: Watts, 1956. 268p.
15. FEUER, LEWIS S., ed. *Marx and Engels: Basic Writings on Politics and Philosophy*. New York: Doubleday, 1959. 497p.
16. RUBEL, MAXIMILIEN, ed. *Pages choises pour une éthique socialiste*. Paris: M. Rivière, 1948. 379p.

17. MARX, KARL, and ENGELS, FRIEDRICH. *The Communist Manifesto*. New York: Russell & Russell, 1963. 365p.
18. ——. *The German Ideology*. New York: International Publishers, 1947. 214p.
19. ——. *The German Ideology*. Moscow: Progress Publishers, 1964. 736p.
20. ——. *The Holy Family*. Moscow: Foreign Languages Publishing House, 1956. 299p.
21. ——. *Letters to Americans, 1848–1895*. New York: International Publishers, 1953. 312p.
22. ——. *Literature and Art*. New York: International Publishers, 1947. 154p.
23. ——. *On Religion*. New York: International Publishers, 1955. 382p.
24. ——. *Selected Correspondence*. Moscow: Foreign Languages Publishing House, 1956. 623p.
25. ——. *Selected Works*. Moscow: Foreign Languages Publishing House, 1950. 2 vols.
26. ——. *Historisch-kritische Gesamtausgabe*. Frankfurt and Moscow: Marx-Engels Institut, 1927–36.
27. ——. *Werke*. Berlin: Dietz, 1957——. 32 vols. to date.
28. MEEK, RONALD L., ed. *Marx and Engels on Malthus*. New York: International Publishers, 1954. 190p.
29. MEHRING, FRANZ, ed. *Aus dem literarischen Nachlass von Karl Marx, Friedrich Engels und Ferdinand Lassalle*. Stuttgart: Dietz, 1902. 4 vols.

30. ENGELS, FRIEDRICH. *Anti-Dühring; Herr Eugen Dühring's Revolution in Science*. Moscow: Foreign Languages Publishing House, 1962. 541 p.

31. ———. *Dialectics of Nature*. New York: International Publishers, 1960. 383p.

32. ———. *Ludwig Feuerbach and the Outcome of Classical German Philosophy*. New York: International Publishers, 1941. 95p.

33. ———. *The Origin of the Family, Private Property and the State*. Moscow: Foreign Languages Publishing House, 1959. 303p.

34. ———. *Socialism, Utopian and Scientific*. Moscow: Foreign Languages Publishing House, 1958. 126p.

35. LENIN, VLADIMIR I. *Collected Works*. Moscow: Foreign Languages Publishing House, 1960——. 42 vols. 1 vol. of index. Translation of the fourth Soviet edition, 35 vols. now complete.

36. ———. *Imperialism, the Highest Stage of Capitalism*. Moscow: Foreign Languages Publishing House, 1947. 154p.

37. ———. *Karl Marx*. Moscow: Foreign Languages Publishing House, 1953. 63p.

38. ———. *Left-Wing Communism, An Infantile Disorder*. Moscow: Foreign Languages Publishing House, 1961. 122p.

39. ———. *Marx, Engels, Marxism*. Moscow: Foreign Languages Publishing House, 1960. 597p.

40. ———. *Materialism and Empirio-Criticism*. New York: International Publishers, 1927. 397p.

41. ———. *On Socialist Ideology and Culture*. Moscow: Foreign Languages Publishing House, 1960. 99p.

42. ———. *One Step Forward, Two Steps Back*. London: Lawrence & Wishart, 1941. 288p.

43. ———. *The Proletarian Revolution and Renegade Kautsky*. New York: International Publishers, 1934. 110p.

44. ———. *Selected Works*. London: Lawrence & Wishart, 1936–39. 12 vols.

45. ———. *Selected Works*. New York: Universal Distributors, 1950. 2 vols.

46. ———. *Socialism and War*. Moscow: Foreign Languages Publishing House, 1952. 94p.

47. ———. *The State*. Moscow: Foreign Languages Publishing House, 1954. 37p.

48. ———. *The State and Revolution.* Moscow: Foreign Languages Publishing House, 195–?. 200p.
49. ———. *The Teachings of Karl Marx.* New York: International Publishers, 1964. 62p.
50. ———. *The Three Sources and Three Component Parts of Marxism.* Moscow: Foreign Languages Publishing House, n.d. 80p.
51. ———. *What Is To Be Done?* Oxford: Clarendon Press, 1963. 213p.
52. ———. *Marxismus und Staat.* Berlin: Dietz, 1960. 143p.
53. ———. *Über die Religion.* Berlin: Dietz, 1956. 94p.

54. STALIN, IOSIF V. *Anarchism or Socialism?* New York: International Publishers, 1953. 64p.
55. ———. *Dialectical and Historical Materialism.* New York: International Publishers, 1940. 48p.
56. ———. *Foundations of Leninism.* New York: International Publishers, 1939. 127p.
57. ———. *Leninism.* New York: International Publishers, 1942. 479p.
58. ———. *Marxism and Linguistics.* New York: International Publishers, 1951. 63p.
59. ———. *Marxism and the National and Colonial Question.* Moscow, Leningrad: Co-operative Publishing Society of Foreign Workers in the U.S.S.R., 1935. 304p.
60. ———. *Marxism vs. Liberalism.* New York: New Century Publishers, 1945. 24p.
61. ———. *The National Question and Leninism.* Moscow: Foreign Languages Publishing House, 1950. 36p.
62. ———. *On Lenin.* Moscow: Foreign Languages Publishing House, 1952. 87p.
63. ———. *Problems of Leninism.* Moscow: Foreign Languages Publishing House, 1947. 642p.
64. ———. *Works.* Moscow: Foreign Languages Publishing House, 1952–55. 13 vols. (incomplete).

65. MAO, TSE-TUNG. *Selected Works.* New York: International Publishers, 1954———. 5 vols.

See also: 497, 932, 933, 944, 1410, 1418, 1420, 1508, 1525, 1545, 1549, 1550, 1554, 1555.

3 ——— THE LIFE AND THOUGHT
OF MARX, ENGELS,
LENIN, AND STALIN

The finest brief intellectual biography of Marx is 67. For
an authoritative biography it is best to consult 81. 79 is by a man
who was for many years a personal friend of Marx. 69 is a study
of Marx's life and thought in the context of the social conditions
of his day. 88 argues that Marx was a neurotic with a severe in-
feriority complex; in spite of this, however, his contribution to
the history of thought is said to be an enduring one. 76 and 89 are
two of the weaker biographies.

66, 68, 73, 77, 84, 92, 115, 123, and 129 are introductory treatments of Marx's life and thought. 71 is a Marxist's paean to work-
ingmen on the greatness of Marx and the truth of his views. Petersen presents a spirited, though not reasoned, defense of Marx
against his "traducers." Other sympathetic accounts are found in
78 and 93. Garaudy writes with greater competence in 72 about
the historical development of Marx's thought. The four most
significant works in this field, however, are 75, 110, 112, and 117.
75 is certainly the best treatment in English of Marx's intellectual
development and of his relation to his predecessors. Rubel's carefully written account (117) is also worthy of study. 112 pays
special attention to the sources of historical materialism from Hegel
to Marx. Calvez's work (109) does not fall far short of the above
four.

Edmund Wilson's work on Marx (102–7) is, at best, spotty.
His occasional flashes of insight may not make the reader feel that
he is adequately compensated for the verbiage. 97 represents an

extreme of simplification; 127 reaches absurd levels of overstatement. In 100 Nomad is successful in discussing Marx's relation to
the key issues and men of his day in a relatively few enlightening
pages. 118 is a serious assessment of Marx as a philosopher; 134
attempts the same task with considerably less success.

In view of the wealth of literature on Marx's life and intellectual
development, it is remarkable that so little is available on Engels.
136 is the best biography we have. 138 tends to overlook weaknesses in viewing Engels through a haze of agreeable sentiment. As
usual, Adler's work (140) has to be taken into serious account.
139 presents an informal discussion of the political circumstances
which prompted Engels to write *Anti-Dühring* as well as a reasoned estimate of the philosophical significance of the work.

Both 145 and 147 are readable and adequate biographies of Lenin.
148 has the advantage (and all the drawbacks) of having been
written by a man who knew Lenin intimately. 144 and 153 present
critical assessments of the foundations of "Leninism." 149 is an
"official" biography of Lenin.

Deutscher's book (154) is perhaps the best on Stalin's thought
and life. 156 is an official biography; to catch a glimpse of the other
side of the story, the reader may investigate 158. Dilas' reports
(155) throw little light on a complex and largely unknown mind.
Surely, an objective reading of Stalin's philosophical work would
not show him worthy of the praise he receives in 159.

66. BEER, MAX. *The Life and Teachings of Karl Marx*. London:
     Allen & Unwin, 1925. 132p.
67. BERLIN, ISAIAH. *Karl Marx*. London: Oxford University Press,
     1948. 280p.
68. BOUQUET, ALAN C. *Karl Marx and his Doctrines*. London:
     S.P.C.K., 1950. 36p.
69. CARR, EDWARD H. *Karl Marx: A Study in Fanaticism*. London:
     Dent, 1934. 315p.
70. CARROLL, L. RAY. *The Pixyllated Prophet*. Billings, Montana:
     The Guardian, 1953. 137p.
71. DANNENBERG, KARL. *Karl Marx; The Man and His Work*. New
     York: The Radical Review Publishing Association, 1918.
     122p.
72. GARAUDY, ROGER. *Karl Marx and His Doctrines*. New York:
     International Publishers, 1965. 256p.

73. GOL'DENDAKH, DAVID B. (RIAZANOV, D., pseud.). *Karl Marx and Friedrich Engels*. New York: International Publishers, 1927. 224p.

74. ———. *Karl Marx, Man, Thinker, and Revolutionist*. London: M. Lawrence, 1927. 282p.

75. HOOK, SIDNEY. *From Hegel to Marx: Studies in the Intellectual Development of Karl Marx*. New York: Humanities Press, 1950. 335p.

76. KORSCH, KARL. *Karl Marx*. New York: Russell & Russell, 1963. 247p.

77. LASKI, HAROLD J. *Karl Marx, an Essay*. London: Allen & Unwin, 1922. 46p.

78. LEWIS, JOHN. *The Life and Teachings of Karl Marx*. London: Lawrence & Wishart, 1965. 286p.

79. LIEBKNECHT, WILHELM. *Karl Marx, Biographical Memoirs*. Chicago: Kerr, 1908. 181p.

80. LORIA, ACHILLE. *Karl Marx*. New York: T. Seltzer, 1920. 163p.

81. MEHRING, FRANZ. *Karl Marx*. New York: Covici, Friede, 1935. 608p.

82. MOSCOW. INSTITUT MARKSIZMA-LENINIZMA. *Reminiscences of Marx and Engels*. Moscow: Foreign Languages Publishing House, 196–?. 402p.

83. NIKOLAEVSKII, BORIS I., and MAENCHEN-HELFEN, OTTO. *Karl Marx, Man and Fighter*. London: Methuen, 1936. 391p.

84. PASCAL, ROY. *Karl Marx: Political Foundations*. London: Labour Monthly Press, 1943. 31p.

85. PERCHIK, LEV M. *Karl Marx*. New York: International Publishers, 1934. 64p.

86. PETERSEN, ARNOLD. *Karl Marx and Marxism*. New York: New York Labor News Co., 1933. 63p.

87. POSTGATE, RAYMOND W. *Karl Marx*. London: H. Hamilton, 1933. 91p.

88. RÜHLE, OTTO. *Karl Marx: His Life and Work*. London: Allen & Unwin, 1929. 419p.

89. SCHWARZSCHILD, LEOPOLD. *The Red Prussian*. New York: Scribner, 1947. 422p.

90. SPARGO, JOHN. *Karl Marx: His Life and Work*. New York: B. W. Huebsch, 1910. 359p.

91. ———. *The Marx He Knew*. Chicago: Kerr, 1909. 85p.

92. SPRIGGE, CECIL J. S. *Karl Marx*. London: Duckworth, 1938. 144p.

93. STEPANOVA, EVGENIIA A. *Karl Marx; Short Biography*. Moscow: Foreign Languages Publishing House, 1960. 150p.

94. COMYN, MARIAN. "My Recollections of Karl Marx," *19th Century and After* 91 (1922), 161–69.

95. HALLETT, JOHN. "Karl Marx: Fifty Years After," *The Fortnightly Review* 139 (1933), 311–21.

96. HAMMEN, OSCAR J. "Capitalizing on *Das Kapital*," *South Atlantic Quarterly* 60 (1961), 19–28.

97. KAY, HUBERT. "Karl Marx," *Life* 25 (October 18, 1948) 63–75.

98. KRIEGER, LEONARD. "Marx and Engels as Historians," *Journal of the History of Ideas* 14 (1953), 381–403.

99. MACIVER, A. M. "Karl Marx," *Sociological Review* 14 (1922), 325–28.

100. NOMAD, MAX. "Karl Marx, the Myth and the Man," *Scribner's Magazine* 93 (March, 1933), 151–54, 186–96.

101. RAPPARD, W. E. "Karl Marx and Labor Legislation," *The Quarterly Journal of Economics* 27 (1913), 530–35.

102. WILSON, EDMUND. "The Emotional Pattern in Marx," *The New Republic* 102 (February 19, 1940), 239–42.

103. ———. "Karl Marx: Poet of Commodities," *The New Republic* 102 (January 8, 1940), 46–47.

104. ———. "Karl Marx: Prometheus and Lucifer," *The New Republic* 95 (July 6, 1938), 244–47.

105. ———. "Marx and Engels: Grinding the Lens," *The New Republic* 96 (September 7, 1938), 125–27.

106. ———. "Marx Decides to Change the World," *The New Republic* 95 (July 20, 1938), 301–4.

107. ———. "The Marx-Engels Partnership," *The New Republic* 96 (August 17, 1938), 40–43.

108. ARON, ROBERT, ed. *De Marx au marxisme*. Paris: Éditions de Flore, 1948. 319p.

109. CALVEZ, JEAN YVES. *La pensée de Karl Marx*. Paris: Éditions du Seuil, 1956. 663p.

110. CORNU, AUGUSTE. *Karl Marx et Friedrich Engels; leur vie et leur oeuvre*. Paris: Presses Universitaires de France, 1955–58. 2 vols.

111. ———. *Karl Marx et la Révolution de 1848*. Paris: Presses Universitaires de France, 1948. 74p.

112. ———. *Karl Marx; l'homme et l'oeuvre*. Paris: Félix Alcan, 1934. 427p.

113. GIGNOUX, CLAUDE J. *Karl Marx*. Paris: Plon, 1950. 259p.
114. KLUGMANN, NARCISSE. *Le prophète rouge; essai sur Marx et le marxisme*. Paris: Les Éditions Rieder, 1938. 367p.
115. RAGON, MICHEL. *Karl Marx*. Paris: Table ronde, 1959. 124p.
116. RUBEL, MAXIMILIEN. *Karl Marx devant le bonapartisme*. Paris: Mouton, 1960. 164p.
117. ———. *Karl Marx, essai de biographie intellectuelle*. Paris: M. Rivière, 1957. 463p.

118. ADLER, MAX. *Marx als Denker*. Berlin: Dietz, 1925. 165p.
119. BERLIN. INSTITUT FÜR MARXISMUS-LENINISMUS. *Karl Marx Album*. Berlin: Dietz, 1953. 147p.
120. BREUER, K. H. *Der junge Marx*. Köln: 1954. 160p.
121. CHAGIN, BORIS A. *Die Entwicklung der marxistischen Philosophie nach der Pariser Kommune (1871–1895)*. Berlin: Verlag Kultur und Fortschritt, 1951. 88p.
122. DRAHN, ERNST. *Marx-Bibliographie: Ein Lebensbild Karl Marx' in biographisch-bibliographischen Daten*. Berlin: Deutsche Verlagsgesellschaft für Politik, 1923. 59p.
123. GROSS, GUSTAV. *Karl Marx*. Leipzig: Duncker und Humblot, 1885. 82p.
124. KOPPEL, AUGUST. *Für und wider Karl Marx*. Karlsruhe: G. Braunsche Hofbuchdruckerei, 1905. 135p.
125. MENDE, GEORG. *Karl Marx' Entwicklung vom revolutionären Demokraten zum Kommunisten*. Berlin: Dietz, 1954. 119p.
126. MILLER, SEPP, und SAWADZKI, BRUNO. *Karl Marx in Berlin*. Berlin: Das Neue Berlin, 1956. 242p.
127. NELKEN, PETER. *Karl Marx, der grösste Sohn des deutschen Volkes*. Berlin: Kongress-Verlag, 1953. 64p.
128. OIZERMAN, T. I. *Die Entstehung der marxistischen Philosophie*. Berlin: Dietz, 1965. 525p.
129. SCHENCK, ERNST VON. *Wer war Karl Marx?* Zollikon: Evangelischer Verlag, 1958. 78p.
130. SCHIEL, HUBERT. *Die Umwelt des jungen Karl Marx*. Trier: J. Lintz, 1954. 36p.
131. TÖNNIES, FERDINAND. *Marx: Leben und Lehre*. Jena: Lichtenstein, 1921.
132. VORLÄNDER, KARL. *Karl Marx: Sein Leben und Sein Werk*. Leipzig: F. Meiner, 1929. 332p.
133. ———. *Marx, Engels und Lassalle als Philosophen*. Berlin: Dietz, 1926. 119p.

134. WERYHA, WLADYSLAW. *Marx als Philosoph*. Bern und Leipzig: A. Siebert, 1894. 52p.
135. WILBRANDT, ROBERT. *Karl Marx: Versuch einer Würdigung*. Leipzig und Berlin: B. G. Teubner, 1920. 135p.

136. MAYER, GUSTAV. *Friedrich Engels*. The Hague: Martinus Nijhoff, 1934. 2 vols.
137. ——. *Friedrich Engels: A Biography*. New York: Knopf, 1936. 332p.
138. STEPANOVA, EVGENIIA A. *Frederick Engels*. Moscow: Foreign Languages Publishing House, 1958. 270p.

139. GOL'DENDAKH, DAVID B. (RIAZANOV, D. pseud.). "On Engels' *Anti-Dühring*," *The Labour Monthly* 2 (1929), 97–106, 171–78.

140. ADLER, MAX. *Engels als Denker*. Berlin: Dietz, 1925. 122p.

141. BUKHARIN, NIKOLAI I. *Lenin as a Marxist*. London: Communist Party of Great Britain, 1925. 64p.
142. FISCHER, LOUIS. *The Life of Lenin*. New York: Harper and Row, 1964. 703p.
143. KRUPSKAIA, NADEZHDA K. *Reminiscences of Lenin*. Moscow: Foreign Languages Publishing House, 1959. 552p.
144. PANNEKOEK, ANTON. *Lenin as Philosopher*. New York: New Essays, 1948. 80p.
145. PAYNE, ROBERT. *The Life and Death of Lenin*. New York: Simon & Schuster, 1964. 672p.
146. POSSONY, STEFAN T. *Lenin: The Compulsive Revolutionary*. Chicago: Regnery, 1964. 418p.
147. SHUB, DAVID. *Lenin*. Garden City, N.Y.: Doubleday, 1951. 438p.
148. TROTSKII, LEV D. *Lenin*. Garden City, N.Y.: Garden City Books, 1959. 216p.
149. *Vladimir I. Lenin; A Political Biography*. New York: International Publishers, 1944. 288p.

150. FITZPATRICK, JOSEPH P., S.J. "Lenin, Heir of Marx," *Thought* 12 (1937), 211–24.
151. NIEMEYER, GERHART. "Lenin and the Total Critique of Society," *The Review of Politics* 26 (1964), 473–504.

152. DRAHN, ERNST. *Lenin, Eine Bio-Bibliographie.* Berlin: R. L. Prager, 1925. 80p.
153. HARPER, J. *Lenin als Philosoph.* Amsterdam: Gruppe Internationaler Kommunisten in Holland, 1938. 112p.

154. DEUTSCHER, ISAAC. *Stalin: A Political Biography.* New York: Vintage Books, 1960. 600p.
155. DJILAS, MILOVAN. *Conversations with Stalin.* New York: Harcourt, Brace and World, 1962. 211p.
156. MOSCOW. INSTITUT MARKSA-ENGEL'SA-LENINA. *Joseph Stalin: A Short Biography.* Moscow: Foreign Languages Publishing House, 1943. 67p.
157. PAYNE, ROBERT. *The Rise and Fall of Stalin.* New York: Simon and Schuster, 1965. 767p.
158. TROTSKII, LEV D. *Stalin: An Appraisal of the Man and His Influence.* New York: Grosset & Dunlap, 1958. 516p.

159. STERN, VIKTOR. *Stalin als Philosoph.* Berlin: Aufbau-Verlag, 1949. 92p.

See also: 361, 404, 740, 869, 870, 883, 900, 909, 940, 966, 968, 971, 988, 991, 1097, 1103, 1187, 1325, 1477.

4 — GENERAL INTRODUCTIONS

There are a large number of works designed to introduce the reader to "Marxism," "Communism" or "dialectical materialism." Most of them are inaccurate, biased, or philosophically ignorant. Few have the structure and clarity necessary for success in the simplified presentation of complex theories; fewer still make any significant contribution to the field. The most useful of the introductions are 202, 209, and 221, though none is a resounding success. Hunt, though he deals with virtually all the important concepts of dialectical materialism, is much better when he writes about social doctrines than when he struggles with metaphysics. Laski's book is a good general account of the Marxist-Leninist philosophy of history, reinforced with occasional glimpses of Communist practice. Other general works which may be worth consulting are 181, 192, 205, 211, 219, 274, 283, 284, 287, 290, 300, 303, 310, 313, 321, and 322.

The bulk of the literature in this section consists of popularizations of the central ideas of dialectical and historical materialism. As might be expected, the popular treatments fall into two separate groups distinguished mainly by the commitments of the authors, not their philosophical competence. On the one hand, 161, 165, 168, 169, 183, 194, 213, 214, 228, 232, 308, and 316 are popular defenses of Marxism. All of these are written with a more or less pronounced partisan bias. Enthusiasm is taken to ridiculous extremes in 231, where Petersen sets out to show that Marx was a philosophical, nay universal, genius. The least inadequate introduction to the Marxist-Leninist view of the development of society by one who believes it is 170. 254 is a defense of Marxism against the "petty-bourgeois" opposition.

On the other hand, we have 163, 177, 179, 201, 206, 210, 236, 241, 248, 254, 255, 268, 318, and 323: all are popular attacks on Marxist philosophy. It is unfortunate that the authors of a number of these critiques begin by admitting that they know little philosophy, but refuse to let this deter them from giving their opinions on philosophical topics. The nadir of reasoning is reached in 164, where the author "proves" that the philosophy of Communism is clearly false by reminding us that it is atheistic, materialistic, and immoral. 258 uses the personal approach to show Marxism-Leninism unworthy of allegiance.

166 abounds in historical information, but both it and 243 are weak on theory. 167 is an expanded dissertation of uneven merit. 172 has a useful and readable account of the flirtation of French intellectuals with dialectical materialism. 173 avoids the most obvious faults of popularization, but its claim that the central error of dialectical materialism is the rejection of the existence of God carries no conviction. Cole's work (174) is the best history of

socialism we have; the student should read it early in his investigations. 175 is a critical study of Marx's views from the socialist standpoint.

188 contains a superficial account of Communism as "a way of life." 184 and 190 are two recent collections which make, in parts, absorbing reading. 190 contains essays by scholars from Eastern as well as Western countries; many make the attempt to utilize the positive elements in Marx. Both 196 and 198 are summary expositions of modest quality. The symposiasts in 200 include Bertrand Russell, John Dewey, and Morris Cohen. Only one section of 183 is about Marxist philosophy, and it is a much simplified account. 212 is a critical look at the fate of Marx's ideas, with some predictions for the future.

For a useful introduction to Marx's socio-economic views the reader may consult 215. 273 views the first volume of *Capital* as a four-act drama rich in symbol and myth. 217 discusses the ideological basis of the Sino-Soviet split. Macek (218) is of the opinion that what Marx really meant is not as significant an issue as how he was understood. Judging by the example of this weak book on the theory and practice of Marxism-Leninism, he was not understood very well. 220 is an attack on Sidney Hook's interpretation of Marxism. Although 222 is not ideal as an introduction, it does give a glimpse of recent thought on a variety of issues. Contributors include Georg Lukács. 224 includes an interesting sociohistorical account of the rise of Marxism-Leninism in Russia. 225, 226, and 247 are books that do not deserve detailed study. 230 is also weak: Parkes's "autopsy" is performed with a dull knife. His judgments concerning the irrelevance of Marxist-Leninist theory and the failure of Soviet practice are hasty and poorly supported. Scott's "anatomy" (244) does not succeed in exposing the conceptual skeleton of Communism.

While 233 is an introductory account of Marxism, Leninism, and Stalinism, 234 deals with Marxist doctrine and its relevance at the time of the Russian Revolution. 237 includes an assessment of our present and future in a world of ideological conflict. 245 construes this ideological conflict, somewhat unconvincingly, as one between idealists and materialists. 252 presents a critical scrutiny of Marxist philosophy, economics, and prophecies, as well as Marxist-Leninist political strategy. Volume 1 of 253 is a reasonably accurate, though not enlightening, exposition of Marxist-Leninist ideology. 250 is positively inaccurate; though designed for high school students, its special appeal is to the dropouts. A very brief sketch of Marxist social theory may be found in 262. 265 argues that all variants of Marxism are failures; 271 dissents by claiming that Marx's social analysis and his humanism are still valid today, even though his economic theory is no longer of value. 286 agrees about the importance of the social analysis of Marxism, but announces its bankruptcy as an ideology.

279 gives a neat and challenging list of the errors of Marxism, not the least of which is a mistaken view of human nature. Heimann maintains (269) that totalitarian collectivism is a natural outcome of Marxian humanism; 293 argues much the same point at greater length. 296 contains a bibliographical introduction to Marxist philosophy. 298 consists of polemical essays by a leading French Marxist. 317, 319, and 320 present critiques of Marxism from the standpoint of national socialism. Of the three, Sombart's work is the most substantial, although it is not one that promotes enlightenment or stimulates insight. Among recent works, 193 is disappointing; 240, though brief, is well worth careful study.

160. ADAMIC, LOUIS. *The Eagle and the Roots*. Garden City, N.Y.: Doubleday, 1952. 531p.
161. AFANAS'EV, VIKTOR G. *Marxist Philosophy: A Popular Outline*. Moscow: Progress Publishers, 1964. 393p.
162. "A STUDENT OF AFFAIRS." *What is Communism?* London: Batchworth Press, 1951. 54p.
163. BALES, JAMES D. *Communism: Its Faith and Fallacies*. Grand Rapids, Mich.: Baker Book House, 1962. 214p.
164. ———. *Understanding Communism*. Grand Rapids, Mich.: Baker Book House, 1962. 88p.
165. BEER, MAX. *A Guide to the Study of Marx*. London: Labor Research Dep't., 1932. 32p.
166. BORKENAU, FRANZ. *World Communism*. Ann Arbor, Mich.: University of Michigan Press, 1962. 444p.
167. BRAMELD, THEODORE B. *A Philosophic Approach to Communism*. Chicago: University of Chicago Press, 1933. 242p.
168. BROWDER, EARL R. *What is Communism?* New York: The Vanguard Press, 1936. 254p.

169. BURNS, EMILE. *An Introduction to Marxism.* London: Lawrence & Wishart, 1957. 75p.
170. ———. *What Is Marxism?* New York: International Publishers, 1957. 91p.
171. CALDWELL, JOHN C. *Communism in Our World.* New York: John Day, 1956. 126p.
172. CAUTE, DAVID. *Communism and the French Intellectuals, 1914–1960.* New York: Macmillan, 1964. 413p.
173. CHAMBRE, HENRI, S. J. *From Karl Marx to Mao Tse-Tung: A Systematic Survey of Marxism-Leninism.* New York: P. J. Kenedy and Sons, 1963. 308p.
174. COLE, GEORGE D. H. *A History of Socialist Thought.* New York: St. Martin's Press, 1953–60. 5 vols.
175. ———. *The Meaning of Marxism.* Ann Arbor, Mich.: University of Michigan Press, 1964. 304p.
176. ———. *What Marx Really Meant.* New York: Knopf, 1934. 309p.
177. COLEGROVE, KENNETH W. *The Menace of Communism.* Princeton, N. J.: Van Nostrand, 1962. 294p.
178. CONWAY, A. W. *Veritas; A Synopsis of Marxian Communism.* Baltimore, Md.: J. H. Furst, 1940. 161p.
179. CRONYN, GEORGE W. *A Primer on Communism: 200 Questions and Answers.* New York: Dutton, 1960. 192p.
180. CROOK, WILFRID H. *Communism and the General Strike.* Hamden, Conn.: Shoe String Press, 1960. 483p.
181. DANIELS, ROBERT V. *The Nature of Communism.* New York: Random House, 1962. 398p.
182. DELEON, DANIEL. *Marx on Mallock.* New York: New York Labor News Co., 1908 (?). 31p.
183. DOBB, MAURICE H. *On Marxism Today.* London: L. and Virginia Woolf at the Hogarth Press, 1932. 48p.
184. DRACHKOVITCH, MILORAD M., ed. *Marxism in the Modern World.* Stanford, Calif.: Stanford University Press, 1965. 293p.
185. [not used]
186. DUNCKER, HERMANN. *Introduction to Marxism.* New York: Universal Distributors, 1962. 283p.
187. DUPRÉ, LOUIS K. *The Philosophical Foundations of Marxism.* New York: Harcourt, Brace and World, 1966. 240p.
188. EBENSTEIN, WILLIAM. *Today's Isms: Communism, Fascism, and Socialism.* New York: Prentice-Hall, 1954. 191p.

189. Fox, Ralph W. *Communism and a Changing Civilisation.* London: John Lane, 1935. 156p.
190. Fromm, Erich, ed. *Socialist Humanism: An International Symposium.* Garden City, N. Y.: Doubleday, 1965. 420p.
191. Gallacher, William. *Marxism and the Working Class.* London: Lawrence & Wishart, 1943. 52p.
192. Golob, Eugene O. *The "Isms": A History and Evaluation.* New York: Harper, 1954. 681p.
193. Gregor, A. James. *A Survey of Marxism: Problems in Philosophy and the Theory of History.* New York: Random House, 1965. 370p.
194. Guest, David A. *Lectures on Marxist Philosophy.* New York: International Publishers, 1963. 90p.
195. Guins, George C. *Communism on the Decline.* The Hague: Martinus Nijhoff, 1956. 287p.
196. Gupta, Kalyan C. *A Critical Examination of Marxist Philosophy.* Calcutta: Privately printed, 1962. 237p.
197. Gurian, Waldemar. *The Rise and Decline of Marxism.* London: Burns, Oates, & Washbourne, 1938. 184p.
198. Hampsch, George H. *The Theory of Communism.* New York: Philosophical Library, 1965. 245p.
199. Hillquit, Morris. *From Marx to Lenin.* New York: Hanford Press, 1921. 151p.
200. Hook, Sidney, ed. *The Meaning of Marx; A Symposium.* New York: Farrar & Rinehart, 1934. 144p.
201. Hoover, J. Edgar. *A Study of Communism.* New York: Holt, Rinehart and Winston, 1962. 212p.
202. Hunt, Robert N. C. *Marxism Past and Present.* New York: Macmillan, 1955. 180p.
203. Il'ichev, L. *Social Progress and Philosophy.* Washington, D.C.: Joint Publications Research Service, 1964. 15p.
204. Kaplan, Abraham. *The New World of Philosophy.* New York: Random House, 1961. 346p.
205. Ketchum, Richard M., ed. *What is Communism?* New York: Dutton, 1955. 191p.
206. Kluckhohn, Frank L. *The Naked Rise of Communism.* Derby, Conn.: Monarch Books, 1962. 286p.
207. Koestler, Arthur. *The Yogi and the Commissar.* New York: Macmillan, 1945. 247p.
208. Landy, A. *Marxism and the Woman Question.* New York: Workers Library Publishers, 1943. 64p.

209. LASKI, HAROLD J. *Communism*. New York: Henry Holt and Co., 1927. 256p.

210. LEFF, GORDON. *The Tyranny of Concepts: A Critique of Marxism*. London: Merlin Press, 1961. 203p.

211. LEITES, NATHAN C. *A Study of Bolshevism*. Glencoe, Ill.: Free Press, 1953. 639p.

212. LE ROSSIGNOL, JAMES E. *From Marx to Stalin: A Critique of Communism*. New York: Crowell, 1940. 442p.

213. LEVY, HYMAN. *A Philosophy for a Modern Man*. New York: Knopf, 1938. 309p.

214. LEWIS, JOHN. *Marxism and Modern Idealism*. London: Lawrence & Wishart, 1944. 43p.

215. LINDSAY, ALEXANDER D. *Karl Marx's CAPITAL: An Introductory Essay*. London: Oxford University Press, 1937. 128p.

216. LOFTHOUSE, WILLIAM F. *The Philosophy of Communism*. London: Epworth Press, 1950. 15p.

217. LOWENTHAL, RICHARD. *World Communism*. New York: Oxford University Press, 1964. 288p.

218. MACEK, JOSEF. *The Impact of Marxism*. Pittsburgh: University of Pittsburgh Press, 1956. 147p.

219. MACMURRAY, JOHN. *The Philosophy of Communism*. London: Faber and Faber, 1933. 96p.

220. MATTICK, PAUL. *The Inevitability of Communism*. New York: Polemic Publishers, 1935. 48p.

221. MAYO, HENRY B. *Introduction to Marxist Theory*. New York: Oxford University Press, 1960. 334p.

222. MILIBAND, RALPH, and SAVILLE, JOHN, eds. *The Socialist Register*. New York: Monthly Review Press, 1965. 362p.

223. MILLER, WILLIAM J., and others. *The Meaning of Communism*. New York: Simon & Schuster, 1964. 192p.

224. MONNEROT, JULES. *Sociology and Psychology of Communism*. Boston: Beacon Press, 1953. 339p.

225. MUKERJI, KRISHNA P. *Marxism*. Colombo: Associated Newspapers of Ceylon, 1946. 73p.

226. MURRY, JOHN M., et al. *Marxism*. London: Chapman & Hall, 1935. 245p.

227. MURRY, JOHN M. *The Necessity of Communism*. London: J. Cape, 1932. 136p.

228. NEEDHAM, JOSEPH. *History Is on Our Side*. New York: Macmillan, 1947. 226p.

229. NICHOLSON, JOSEPH S. *The Revival of Marxism*. London: J. Murray, 1920. 145p.

230. PARKES, HENRY B. *Marxism: an Autopsy*. Boston: Houghton Mifflin, 1939. 300p.

231. PETERSEN, ARNOLD. *Karl Marx and Marxian Science*. New York: Labor News Press, 1943. 190p.

232. ———. *Marxism vs. Anti-Marxism*. New York: New York Labor News, 1931. 30p.

233. PLAMENATZ, JOHN P. *From Marx to Stalin*. London: Batchworth Press, 1953. 48p.

234. ———. *What is Communism?* London: National News-Letter, 1947. 120p.

235. PLEKHANOV, GEORGII V. *Fundamental Problems of Marxism*. London: M. Lawrence, 1929. 145p.

236. PORTER, EUGENE O. *Fallacies of Karl Marx*. El Paso, Texas: Texas Western College, 1962. 96p.

237. POSNACK, EMANUEL R. *World Without Barriers*. New York: Morrow, 1956. 434p.

238. READ, HERBERT E. *Essential Communism*. London: S. Nott, 1935. 32p.

239. ROGERS, EDWARD. *A Commentary on Communism*. London: Epworth Press, 1951. 238p.

240. ROTENSTREICH, NATHAN. *Basic Problems of Marx's Philosophy*. New York: Bobbs-Merrill, 1965. 168p.

241. SAAR, ROBERT J. *The Fallacy of Communism*. Boston: Meador Pub., 1956. 119p.

242. SABINE, GEORGE H. *Marxism*. Ithaca, N.Y.: Cornell University Press, 1958. 60p.

243. SALVADORI, MASSIMO. *The Rise of Modern Communism*. New York: Holt, 1952. 176p.

244. SCOTT, ANDREW M. *The Anatomy of Communism*. New York: Philosophical Library, 1951. 197p.

245. SEELY, CHARLES S. *Philosophy and the Ideological Conflict*. New York: Philosophical Library, 1953. 319p.

246. SELSAM, HOWARD. *Philosophy in Revolution*. New York: International Publishers, 1957. 160p.

247. ———. *What is Philosophy? A Marxist Introduction*. New York: International Publishers, 1962. 190p.

248. SPRATT, PHILIP. *A New Look at Marx*. London: Phoenix House, 1957. 52p.

249. STOCKHAMMER, MORRIS, ed. *Karl Marx Dictionary*. New York: Philosophical Library, 1965. 273p.

250. SWEARINGEN, RODGER. *The World of Communism*. Boston: Houghton Mifflin, 1962. 278p.

251. TROTSKII, LEV D. *In Defense of Marxism*. New York: Pioneer Publishers, 1942. 211p.

252. TURNER, JOHN K. *Challenge to Karl Marx*. New York: Reynal and Hitchcock, 1941. 455p.

253. UNITED STATES CONGRESS. HOUSE COMMITTEE ON UN-AMERICAN ACTIVITIES. *Facts on Communism*. Washington: U.S. Government Printing Office, 1959. 2 vols.

254. UNITED STATES CONGRESS. HOUSE COMMITTEE ON UN-AMERICAN ACTIVITIES. *The Ideological Fallacies of Communism*. Washington: U.S. Government Printing Office, 1957. 25p.

255. UNITED STATES CONGRESS. SENATE COMMITTEE ON THE JUDICIARY. *Contradictions of Communism*. Washington: U.S. Government Printing Office, 1959. 54p.

256. WATON, HARRY. *The Philosophy of Marx*. New York: The Marx Institute, 1921. 268p.

257. WEST, ALICK. *Crisis and Criticism*. London: Lawrence & Wishart, 1937. 199p.

258. WHY I OPPOSE COMMUNISM: A SYMPOSIUM. By Bertrand Russell and others. London: Phoenix House, 1956. 54p.

259. WOLFE, BERTRAM D. *Marxism: One Hundred Years in the Life of a Doctrine*. New York: Dial, 1965. 325p.

260. WOOLF, LEONARD S. *Barbarians Within and Without*. New York: Harcourt, Brace, 1939. 180p.

261. ZETKIN, KLARA. *Lenin on the Woman's Question*. New York: International Publishers, 1934. 31p.

262. BOBER, M. M. "Outlines of Marxism," *Education* 60 (1940), 410–15.

263. BROWN, WILLIAM. "The Psychology of Ideological Conflict," *The Fortnightly Review* 174 (1950), 285–91.

264. BURNS, EMILE. "Marxism Revisited: A Communist Reply," *The New Statesman and Nation* 45 (1953), 694–95.

265. COREY, LEWIS. "Marxism Reconsidered," *Nation* 150 (1940), 245–48, 272–75, 305–7.

266. EASTMAN, MAX. "Trotsky Becomes a Scholastic," *Southern Review* 6 (1940), 317–35.

267. ENSOR, ROBERT C. K. "What Marxism Is," *Spectator* 150 (1933), 636–37.

268. HALLE, LOUIS J. "Truth versus Ideology," *The New Republic* 144 (1961): I. "Truth versus Ideology" (May 15), 12–14; II. "What We Are Fighting" (May 22), 18–20; III. "The Two Maps" (May 29), 11–13.

269. HEIMANN, EDUARD. "Marxism: 1848 and 1948," *The Journal of Politics* 11 (1949), 523–31.
270. HOOK, SIDNEY. "On the Battlefield of Philosophy," *Partisan Review* 16 (1949), 251–68.
271. ———. "What's Left of Karl Marx?" *Saturday Review of Literature* 42 (June 6, 1959), 12–14.
272. ———. "What is Living and What is Dead in Marxism," *Southern Review* 6 (1940), 293–316.
273. HYMAN, STANLEY E. "*Capital* as Literature," *Kenyon Review* 23 (1961), 590–610.
274. JONES, LLEWELLYN. "What Did Marx Really Mean?" *Christian Century* 50 (1933), 456–58.
275. KAMENKA, EUGENE. "The Baptism of Karl Marx," *The Hibbert Journal* 56 (1958), 340–51.
276. KUHN, WILLIAM F. "Fifty Years After," *Thought* 8 (1933–34), 459–70.
277. LERNER, ABBA P. "From Vulgar Political Economy to Vulgar Marxism," *The Journal of Political Economy* 47 (1939), 557–67.
278. ———. "Marxism and Economics: Sweezy and Robinson," *The Journal of Political Economy* 53 (1945), 79–87.
279. LERNER, MAX. "Six Errors of Marxism," *The New Republic* 97 (1938–39), 37–38.
280. MILLS, FREDERICK C. "Opening Remarks," *American Economics Review* 39 (1949), 13–15.
281. NEILL, THOMAS P. "Marx and the Modern Mind," *Catholic World* 164 (1947), 395–401.
282. NIEBUHR, REINHOLD. "Marxism in Eclipse," *Spectator* 170 (1943), 518–19.
283. PEARCE, G. J. M. "Marxism," *Church Quarterly Review* 145 (1947), 66–79.
284. POLANYI, MICHAEL. "The Magic of Marxism," *Encounter* 7 (December, 1956), 5–17.
285. RIGNANO, EUGENIO. "Marxists at the Cross-Roads," *Economic Journal* 30 (1920), 408–11.
286. SILONE, IGNAZIO. "Marxism from Another Angle," *The Commonweal* 48 (1948), 521–23.
287. STRACHEY, JOHN. "Marxism Revisited," *The New Statesman and Nation* 45 (1953): I. (May 2), 508–9; II. (May 9), 537–8; III. (May 16), 571–2; IV. (May 23), 602–4.
288. WILLIAMS, RAYMOND. "The Future of Marxism," *The Twentieth Century* 170 (1961), 128–42.

289. WILSON, EDMUND. "Marxist Humanism," *The New Republic* 98 (1939), 371–72.

290. BAAS, ÉMILE. *L'humanisme marxiste; essai d'analyse critique.* Colmar: Éditions Alsatia, 1947. 101p.

291. BÉRACHA, SAMMY. *Le marxisme après Marx.* Paris: Marcel Rivière, 1937. 221p.

292. BLOCK, MAURICE. *Karl Marx; fictions et paradoxes.* Paris: V. Giard & E. Brière, 1900. 19p.

293. COLLINET, MICHEL. *La tragédie du marxisme.* Paris: Calmann-Lévy, 1948. 337p.

294. CORNU, AUGUSTE. *Essai de critique marxiste.* Paris: Éditions sociales, 1951. 187p.

295. ———. *Karl Marx et la pensée moderne.* Paris: Éditions sociales, 1948. 190p.

296. DESROCHES, HENRI-CHARLES. *Signification du marxisme.* Paris: Éditions ouvrières, 1949. 397p.

297. FOUGEYROLLAS, PIERRE. *Le marxisme en question.* Paris: Éditions du Seuil, 1959. 172p.

298. GARAUDY, ROGER. *Humanisme marxiste.* Paris: Éditions sociales, 1957. 311p.

299. ———. *Le communisme et la renaissance de la culture française.* Paris: Éditions sociales, 1945. 63p.

300. LAURAT, LUCIEN. *Le marxisme en faillite? Du marxisme de Marx au marxisme d'aujourd'hui?* Paris: Pierre Tisué, 1939. 268p.

301. LEFÈBVRE, HENRI. *Le marxisme.* Paris: Presses Universitaires de France, 1948. 127p.

302. LE MARXISME-LÉNINISME (no author). Paris: Le Cité catholique, 1960. 399p.

303. LEPP, IGNACE. *Le marxisme, philosophie imbigue et efficace.* Paris: Labergerie, 1949. 342p.

304. MAILLARD, PIERRE. *Du skepticisme au marxisme.* Paris: Picart, 1937. 215p.

305. MAULNIER, THIERRY. *La pensée marxiste.* Paris: A. Fayard, 1948. 223p.

306. RENNES, JACQUES. *Du marxisme à l'humanisme.* Paris: L'Amitie par le livre, 1946. 192p.

307. ———. *Exposé du marxisme.* Paris: Éditions Liberté, 1934. 226p.

308. ADLER, MAX. *Der Marxismus als proletarische Lebens-lehre.* Berlin: E. Laub, 1923. 57p.

309. ———. *Über psychologische und ethische "Läuterung" des Marxismus*. Berlin: E. Laub, 1928. 44p.

310. KHARASOV, GEORG. *Das System des Marxismus*. Berlin: H. Bondy, 1910. 347p.

311. KORSCH, KARL. *Marxismus und Philosophie*. Leipzig: Hirschfeld Verlag, 1930. 160p.

312. KUCZYNSKI, JÜRGEN. *Zurück zu Marx!* Leipzig: C. L. Hirschfeld, 1926. 217p.

313. LIEBER, HANS J. *Die Philosophie des Bolschewismus in den Grundzügen ihrer Entwicklung*. Frankfurt am Main: M. Diesterweg, 1958. 107p.

314. MAYER, HANS. *Karl Marx und das Elend des Geistes*. Meisenheim am Glan: A. Hain, 1948. 107p.

315. MOSZKOWSKA, NATALIE. *Das Marxsche System*. Berlin: H. R. Engelmann, 1929. 190p.

316. OELSSNER, FRED. *Der Marxismus der Gegenwart und seine Kritiker*. Berlin: Dietz, 1952. 336p.

317. RENZ, OTTO. *Der Marxismus*. München: F. Eher, 1931. 36p.

318. SALTER, ERNEST J., und THOMAS, STEPHAN. *Taschenbuch des Kommunismus in These und Gegenthese*. Bad Godesberg: Hohwacht Verlag, 1963. 236p.

319. SCHULZ, FRITZ O. H. *Untergang des Marxismus*. Stuttgart: J. Engelhorn, 1933. 371p.

320. SOMBART, WERNER. *Der proletarische Sozialismus ("Marxismus")*. Jena: G. Fischer, 1924. 2 vols.

321. THEIMER, WALTER. *Der Marxismus*. Bern: A. Francke, 1950. 252p.

322. TUGAN-BARANOVSKII, MIKHAIL I. *Theoretische Grundlagen des Marxismus*. Leipzig: Duncker & Humblot, 1905. 239p.

323. WEISENGRUEN, PAUL. *Das Ende des Marxismus*. Leipzig: O. Wigand, 1899. 80p.

See also: 419, 422, 724, 725, 732, 745, 930, 1209, 1225, 1239, 1242, 1246, 1258, 1409, 1423, 1424.

5 ——————— MARXIST PHILOSOPHY AND THE HISTORY OF THOUGHT

This section contains works that fall into two broad groups. To the first group belong books and articles that explore the historical connections or the logical similarities between dialectical and historical materialism and other major philosophical theories. The second group consists of assessments by Marxists of some major figures and movements in the history of thought.

In the first group the relation of dialectical materialism to the theories of Hegel and Feuerbach has received especially close scrutiny. 330 and 336 explore the philosophical influences that shaped the thought of Marx, with special emphasis on these two figures. The second part of 343 is a good general treatment of the development of European thought after Hegel. 377 is a provocative argument designed to identify the Marxian counterpart of Hegel's concept of the cunning of reason. 379 compares Marx's views of God, man, and nature in his early work with those of Hegel, Schleiermacher, and Feuerbach. 397 is a well-written account of the development of dialectical materialism in its nineteenth-century intellectual context. 394 is a critical study of the Marxist worldview; 395 presents a useful, though by no means exhaustive, examination of the antecedents of dialectical materialism from the Reformation through Spinoza to Hegel. Other works on the relation of dialectical materialism to Hegel's thought include 328, 381, 382, 391, 392, 393, 401, and 412.

The relation of dialectical materialism to the philosophy of Spinoza is discussed in 408 and is briefly touched upon in 395. 341

is a series of essays by Soviet philosophers on Spinoza. Although these essays are, on occasion, insightful, they fall far short of an adequate assessment of the connection between Spinoza and Marx. Much still remains to be done on the relation of Marxist philosophy to the philosophy of Kant as well. The least inadequate treatments are 388 and 410. 409 and 389 contain no more than undeveloped hints. 344 contains two chapters comparing Marx's social theories with those of Rousseau. According to Murry, one of the fatal shortcomings of Marxism is its blindness to moral distinctions. Rousseau's relation to Marx is also discussed in 389 and 405. In addition to the dialectical materialist evaluations in 346 and 356, Dewey's relation to Marx is treated, without spectacular success, in 358 and 368.

From among Marx's contemporaries 339, 384, and 405 select Proudhon for special attention. Marx's relation to the anarchist Bakunin is discussed informatively in 327, passionately in 340. 352 is a clear-headed, though in places superficial, examination of the principles of socialism, anarchism, and syndicalism; 366 is a suggestive treatment of the influence of Bakunin on some variants of Marxism. Bakunin's work (324) is included for the light it throws, both by contrast and by direct statement, on the principles of historical materialism. An elementary but important note about Marx's relation to Darwin is Hook's reminder (367) that the theory of the class struggle was not a result of applying to society the idea of the struggle for survival. 326 is an overrated work: it abounds in vague generalities and hazy labels. 338 and 369 are tangled studies of Darwin, Marx, Frazer, and Freud. The connections between these four thinkers deserve more careful and more precise scrutiny. 334 is a weak treatment of Marx, Freud, and Einstein.

The issue of the relation of dialectical materialism to existentialism is of growing current interest. It is ably handled in 345 and 374. 383 is a leading Marxist's powerful, though partisan, plea. 332 and 372 are important for the student interested in Sartre. 325 is an imaginative translation of Marx's theory of value into Aristotelian terms, with a view to providing the ontological basis of the Marxist economic theories. 342 is an inaccurate study of such figures as Kant, Marx, and Sartre. Gregor's provocative article (364) is designed to show that Gentile's interpretation of Marx is essentially correct: Marx's materialism is simply insistence on the primacy of "sensuous practice." 370 is an interesting and well-written account of the influence of Marx on the political views and literary works of Shaw. 371 is a refutation of Marx's charge that Aristotle had no theory of value. 373 presents a nebulous argument to show that Marxists confuse the "order of reality" with the "order of logic."

The second group of works included in this section suffers too frequently from the attempt to gain insight into a philosophy or to dismiss it on the basis of showing its relation to the socio-economic conditions of its day. Perhaps the most successful practitioner of this art of correlating the ideological superstructure with the economic base is Lukács in such a book as 399. 400, although it shows immense learning, is less convincing. In the case of Plato (357), the method still yields some results. In 356, however, it has lost its plausibility, and in 346 it approaches total insignificance.

For the "official" Marxist view of virtually any thinker in the history of philosophy the reader may consult 390. 355 presents Marxist studies of early Greek philosophy; 349 is a very able interpretation of the materialism of Holbach, Helvetius, and Marx. 406 contains some solid scholarly work. 329 is a Marxist critique of current linguistic analysis, along with a general defense of the legitimacy of philosophical thought.

The number of significant topics in the field covered by this section, on which there is little or no literature in English, French, or German, staggers the imagination. There is considerably more available in Russian, but the work of Soviet historians of philosophy and historians of ideas remains, for the most part, untranslated. Competent Marxist studies of major thinkers might make substantial contributions to our understanding of them. Yet until today only a relatively small proportion of major philosophers has attracted the serious and sustained scrutiny of Western Marxists. Competent examination of the relation of dialectical materialism to other major philosophical systems might conduce to a better understanding and sounder evaluation of it. Yet until today some of the most obvious lines of investigation have remained unexplored by Marxists in the West. I shall mention only two examples. Little has been done to examine the central Marxian notion of production in the context of the Aristotelian concepts of process and activity, which have played a decisive role in much of Western philosophy. Even less serious work has gone into the comparison of the Marxist idea of the second stage of Communist society with various other conceptions of Utopia. It is to be hoped that the current increase of philosophical interest in dialectical and historical materialism will bring with it a wealth of scholarly studies. In the meantime, there are many topics for exploration by doctoral candidates both in philosophy and in the history of ideas.

324. BAKUNIN, MIKHAIL A. *The Political Philosophy of Bakunin: Scientific Anarchism.* New York: Free Press, 1964. 434p.
325. BALZ, ALBERT G. A. *The Value Doctrine of Karl Marx.* New York: King's Crown Press, 1943. 49p.
326. BARZUN, JACQUES. *Darwin, Marx, Wagner: Critique of a Heritage.* Boston: Little, Brown and Company, 1941. 420p.
327. CARR, EDWARD H. *Michael Bakunin.* London: Macmillan, 1937. 501p.
328. COOPER, REBECCA. *The Logical Influence of Hegel on Marx.* U. of Washington Publications in the Social Sciences, Vol. II. Seattle: University of Washington Press, 1925. 182p.
329. CORNFORTH, MAURICE. *Marxism and Linguistic Philosophy.* New York: International Publishers, 1966. 384p.
330. CORNU, AUGUSTE. *The Origins of Marxian Thought.* Springfield, Ill.: C. C. Thomas, 1957. 128p.
331. DELEON, DANIEL. *James Madison and Karl Marx; A Contrast and a Similarity.* New York: National Executive Committee of the Socialist Labor Party, 1920. 30p.
332. DESAN, WILFRED. *The Marxism of Jean-Paul Sartre.* Garden City, N. Y.: Doubleday, 1965. 320p.
333. DOBRIN, SAMUEL. *Lenin and Anarchism.* Oxford, England: St. Antony's College, 1957. 17p.
334. FREEHOF, SOLOMON B. *Marx, Freud and Einstein.* Chicago: The Argus Book Shop, 1933. 46p.
335. GRAY, ALEXANDER. *The Socialist Tradition: Moses to Lenin.* New York: Longmans, Green, 1946. 523p.
336. HOOK, SIDNEY. *Towards the Understanding of Karl Marx.* New York: John Day, 1933. 347p.
337. HUMMERT, PAUL A. *Marxist Elements in the Works of George B. Shaw.* Ann Arbor, Mich.: University Microfilms, 1953.
338. HYMAN, STANLEY E. *The Tangled Bank.* New York: Atheneum, 1962. 492p.

339. JACKSON, JOHN H. *Marx, Proudhon, and European Socialism.*
     New York: Macmillan, 1958. 192p.
340. KENAFICK, K. J. *Michael Bakunin and Karl Marx.* Melbourne:
     A. Maller, 1948. 384p.
341. KLINE, GEORGE L., ed. and trans. *Spinoza in Soviet Philoso-
     phy.* London: Routledge and K. Paul, 1952. 190p.
342. LUIJPEN, W. A. *Phenomenology and Atheism.* Pittsburgh:
     Duquesne University Press, 1964. 344p.
343. MARCUSE, HERBERT. *Reason and Revolution: Hegel and the
     Rise of Social Theory.* Boston: Beacon Press, 1960. 431p.
344. MURRY, JOHN M. *Heroes of Thought.* New York: Messner,
     1938. 368p.
345. ODAJNYK, WALTER. *Marxism and Existentialism.* New York:
     Doubleday Anchor Books, 1965. 211p.
346. OKUN, SID. *John Dewey, A Marxian Critique.* Chicago: Revo-
     lutionary Workers League, 1942. 25p.
347. PANNEKOEK, ANTON. *Marxism and Darwinism.* Chicago: Kerr,
     1912. 58p.
348. PLAINE, HENRY L., ed. *Darwin, Marx, and Wagner: A Sym-
     posium.* Columbus, Ohio: Ohio State University Press,
     1962. 165p.
349. PLEKHANOV, GEORGII V. *Essays in the History of Materialism.*
     London: John Lane, 1934. 287p.
350. ———. *Utopian Socialism of the 19th Century.* Moscow: For-
     eign Languages Publishing House, 1959. 79p.
351. READ, HERBERT E. *Existentialism, Marxism, and Anarchism.*
     London: Freedom Press, 1949. 56p.
352. RUSSELL, BERTRAND. *Roads to Freedom.* London: Allen &
     Unwin, 1919. 215p.
353. SHAW, GEORGE B. *Bernard Shaw and Karl Marx, A Sympo-
     sium.* New York: Random House, 1930. 200p.
354. *A Soviet History of Philosophy: The Outline of a New Vol-
     ume.* William Edgerton, trans. Washington, D.C.: Public
     Affairs Press, 1950. 58p.
355. THOMSON, GEORGE D. *The First Philosophers.* New York:
     International Publishers, 1955. 367p.
356. WELLS, HARRY K. *Pragmatism: Philosophy of Imperialism.*
     New York: International Publishers, 1954. 221p.
357. WINSPEAR, ALBAN D. *The Genesis of Plato's Thought.* New
     York: S. A. Russell, 1956. 390p.

358. CORK, JIM. "John Dewey, Karl Marx and Democratic Social-
     ism," *Antioch Review* 9 (1949), 435–52.

359. DEWEY, ERNEST W., and MILLER, D. L. "Veblen's Naturalism versus Marxian Materialism," *Southwestern Social
Science Quarterly* 35 (1954), 165–74.

360. DWORKIN, GERALD. "Marx and Mill: A Dialogue," *Philosophy
and Phenomenological Research* 26 (1966), 403–14.

361. FEUER, LEWIS S. "The Influence of the American Communist
Colonies on Engels and Marx," *Western Political Quarterly* 19 (1966), 456–74.

362. ———. "John Stuart Mill and Marxian Socialism," *Journal
of the History of Ideas* 10 (1949), 297–303.

363. FLETCHER, JOHN G. "Spengler, Marx and Keyserling; Three
Visions of History," *Living Age* 333 (1927), 723–27.

364. GREGOR, A. JAMES. "Giovanni Gentile and the Philosophy of
the Young Karl Marx," *Journal of the History of Ideas* 24
(1963), 213–30.

365. GROSSMAN, HENRY K. "The Evolutionist Revolt against Classical Economics," Part II: "In England—James Stewart,
Richard Jones, Karl Marx," *Journal of Political Economy*
51 (1943), 506–22.

366. HODGES, DONALD C. "Bakunin's Controversy with Marx; an
Analysis of the Tensions Within Modern Socialism,"
American Journal of Economics 19 (1960), 259–74.

367. HOOK, SIDNEY. "Marx and Darwinism," *The New Republic*
67 (July 29, 1931), 290.

368. ———. "Marx, Dewey and Lincoln," *The New Leader* 40
(October 21, 1957), 16–18.

369. HYMAN, STANLEY E. "After the Great Metaphors," *The
American Scholar* 31, (1962), 236–58.

370. IRVINE, WILLIAM. "George Bernard Shaw and Karl Marx,"
The Journal of Economic History 6 (1946), 53–72.

371. JOHNSON, VAN. "Aristotle's Theory of Value," *American
Journal of Philology* 60 (1939), 445–51.

372. LICHTHEIM, GEORGE. "Sartre, Marxism, and History," *History and Theory* 3 (1963–64), 222–46.

373. McCOY, CHARLES N. R. "Logical and the Real in Political
Theory: Plato, Aristotle, and Marx," *American Political
Science Review* 48 (1954), 1058–66.

374. OLAFSON, FREDERICK A. "Existentialism, Marxism and Historical Justification," *Ethics* 65 (1954–55), 126–34.

375. PASCAL, ROY, and PASCAL, FANIA. "Hegel's Philosophy of
Right and His Importance for Marx," *Labour Monthly* 25
(1943), 285–88.

376. Rosenberg, Bernard. "Veblen and Marx," *Social Research* 15 (1948), 99–117.

377. Tucker, Robert C. "The Cunning of Reason in Hegel and Marx," *The Review of Politics* 18 (1956), 269–95.

378. Berth, Édouard. *Du "Capital" aux "Réflexions sur la violence."* Paris: M. Rivière, 1932. 272p.

379. Cottier, Georges M. *L'Athéisme du jeune Marx: ses origines hégéliennes.* Paris: J. Vrin, 1959. 384p.

380. Grégoire, Franz. *Aux sources de la pensée de Marx: Hegel, Feuerbach.* Louvain: Institut Supérieur de Philosophie, 1947. 204p.

381. Hyppolite, Jean. *Études sur Marx et Hegel.* Paris: M. Rivière, 1955. 204p.

382. Leseine, Leopold. *L'influence de Hegel sur Marx.* Paris: Bonvalot-Jouve, 1907. 257p.

383. Lukács, György. *Existentialisme ou marxisme?* Paris: Nagel, 1961. 290p.

384. Raphael, Max. *Proudhon, Marx, Picasso.* Paris: Éditions Excelsior, 1953. 237p.

385. Sorel, Georges. *D'Aristote à Marx.* Paris: M. Rivière, 1935. 275p.

386. Cuvillier, Armand. "Durkheim et Marx," *Cahiers Internationaux de Sociologie* 4 (1948), 75–97.

387. Haubtmann, Pierre. " 'Forces productives' et 'Forces collectives'," *Cahiers Internationaux de Sociologie* 4 (1948), 135–52.

388. Adler, Max. *Kant und der Marxismus.* Berlin: E. Laub, 1925. 247p.

389. ——. *Wegweiser; Studien zur Geistesgeschichte des Sozialismus.* Berlin & Stuttgart: Dietz, 1923. 248p.

390. Akademiia Nauk SSSR. Institut Filosofii. *Geschichte der Philosophie.* Berlin: Deutscher Verlag der Wissenschaften, 1959——. 5 vols.

391. Bekker, Konrad. *Marx' Philosophische Entwicklung: Sein Verhältnis zu Hegel.* Basel: Volksdruckerei, 1940. 134p.

392. Buggenhagen, Erick A. von. *Die Stellung zur Wirklichkeit bei Hegel und Marx.* Radolfzell: Dressler, 1933. 74p.

393. Haus, Rudolf. *Hegel oder Marx?* Berlin: A. Schultz, 1931. 95p.

394. HELANDER, SVEN. *Marx und Hegel.* Jena: G. Fischer, 1922. 84p.
395. KÖHLER, HANS. *Gründe des dialektischen Materialismus in europäischen Denken.* München: Anton Pustet, 1961. 206p.
396. LEICH, HELMUT G. R. *Die anthropologisch-soziologische Methodik bei Karl Marx, Werner Sombart und Max Weber.* Köln: Privately printed, 1957. 207p.
397. LÖWITH, KARL. *Von Hegel bis Nietzsche.* Zürich: Europa Verlag, 1941. 538p.
398. LUKÁCS, GYÖRGY. *Der junge Hegel: Über die Beziehungen von Dialektik und Ökonomie.* Zürich: Europa Verlag, 1948. 720p.
399. ———. *Der junge Hegel und die Probleme der kapitalistischen Gesellschaft.* Berlin: Aufbau-Verlag, 1948. 654p.
400. ———. *Die Zerstörung der Vernunft.* Berlin: Aufbau-Verlag, 1954. 692p.
401. PLENGE, JOHANN. *Marx und Hegel.* Tübingen: H. Lauppsche Buchhandlung, 1911. 184p.
402. REDING, MARCEL. *Thomas von Aquin und Karl Marx.* Graz: Akademische Druck und Verlagsanstalt, 1953. 22p.
403. SANNWALD, ROLF. *Marx und die Antike.* Zürich: Polygraphischer Verlag, 1957. 210p.
404. SCHUFFENHAUER, WERNER. *Feuerbach und der junge Marx.* Berlin: Deutscher Verlag der Wissenschaften, 1965. 231p.
405. SEILLIÈRE, ERNEST A. *Der demokratische Imperialismus.* Berlin: H. Barsdorf, 1907. 438p.
406. STIEHLER, GOTTFRIED, ed. *Beiträge zur Geschichte des vormarxistischen Materialismus.* Berlin: Dietz, 1961. 310p.
407. ———. *Die Dialektik in Hegels "Phänomenologie des Geistes."* Berlin: Akademie Verlag, 1964. 316p.
408. THALHEIMER, AUGUST. *Spinozas Stellung in der Vorgeschichte des dialektischen Materialismus.* Wien: Verlag für Literatur und Politik, 1928. 118p.
409. VORLÄNDER, KARL. *Kant und der Sozialismus, unter besonderer Berücksichtigung der neuesten theoretischen Bewegung innerhalb des Marxismus.* Berlin: Reuther & Reichard, 1900. 69p.
410. ———. *Kant und Marx; Ein Beitrag zur Philosophie des Sozialismus.* Tübingen: Mohr, 1926. 328p.
411. WEBER, MARIANNE. *Fichte's Sozialismus und sein Verhältnis zur Marxschen Doktrin.* Tübingen: Mohr, 1900. 122p.
412. WETTER, GUSTAV A. *Die Umkehrung Hegels: Grundzüge*

und Ursprünge der Sowjetphilosophie. Köln: Verlag Wissenschaft und Politik, 1963. 93p.

413. ZELENY, J. "Kant und Marx als Kritiker der Vernunft," *Kant-Studien* 56 (1966), 329–41.

See also: 9, 20, 29, 32, 69, 72, 75, 81, 100, 117, 174, 182, 295, 502, 517, 521, 530, 541, 543, 559, 615, 654, 670, 685, 856, 878, 881, 884, 898, 918, 943, 949, 961, 969, 975, 998, 1008, 1102, 1123, 1149, 1316, 1390, 1428, 1429.

6 — DIALECTICAL MATERIALISM

For a provocative, short, general account of the origins and nature of dialectical materialism the reader might consult 443. It includes a discussion of such central concepts as those of matter, cause, and perception. 422 is perhaps the best introduction by a Marxist. The best extended treatment of Marxism-Leninism as a total philosophy, however, is 414. It includes a lucid exposition and perceptive critique of Marxist metaphysics, epistemology, ethics, and philosophy of history. 419 is a sober attempt by a British socialist to identify the significant and enduring elements of Marxism. 426 includes a searching examination of dialectical materialism and the laws of the dialectic. 450 discusses the nature of materialism in the context of Indian views; 444 presents a general study of materialism, which is useful for an understanding of Marx's view.

There is a large number of introductions to dialectical materialism by philosophers who take a partisan interest in making it appear plausible or true. Of these 415, 435, and 437 distinguish themselves as uncommonly dull repetitions of the fundamental tenets and practical significance of the view. 434, 465, 475, 484, and 487 place special stress on the close connection between the theory of dialectical materialism and its practical application. 477 goes so far as to suggest that the theory and its proper application solve all social and personal problems. 420, 471, 472, and 488 are rudimentary; 421, 468, 473, 476, and 479 are somewhat tighter and more comprehensive in their exposition of Marxist theory. 457 is largely polemical in character. 441 is a philosophically garbled defense of dialectical materialism as a consistent and adequate philosophy. 430 is a collection of essays, mostly by Marxists, about some of the principles and about the validity of dialectical materialism. While 449 is a philosophically ignorant attack on Sidney Hook's evaluation of Marxism-Leninism, 453 is a withering rejoinder to Eastman on behalf of the Marxian dialectic.

On the other side we have a series of elementary works on dialectical materialism by philosophers who go to some pains to demonstrate its weaknesses or falsity. 431, 455, 456, 464, 478, 481, and 486 belong in this group. Sorel's work on the collapse of Marxism (463) is unconvincing; 489 is not up to Wetter's best work. 440 is a loose polemical piece in which Eastman argues that dialectical materialism is metaphysics, not science. 439, 442, 447, 448, and 454 are contributions to a discussion of dialectical materialism in *The Labour Monthly*. The debate began with two unimpressive critical articles by Carritt (439); it continued on the same uninspired level with 442 and 454. 447 (435 in its original form) was designed as a major statement to counter 439. It is a showpiece of bad reasoning. 448 draws the important distinction between contradiction and antagonism.

416 is a reprint of the Winter 1948 issue of *Science and Society* and contains a number of articles of general interest. 417 is a translation of a portion of the Soviet Academy of Science's Memorial Volume on the fiftieth anniversary of Marx's death. It contains articles, among others, on the bearing of dialectical materialism on the physical and social sciences. 428 is a translation of papers read by Soviet philosophers at the Twelfth International Congress of Philosophy. 424 undertakes to study Sidney Hook's views on Marxism. 425 is a collection of essays by various hands on the theory and practice of Communism; 429 is another collection, read at the Pontifical Academy of St. Thomas in Rome. Horowitz's book (427) contains a vigorous attack on Sorel's attack on Marxism.

For one of the rare discussions of the dialectical materialist philosophy of mind, the reader is advised to consult 432. A group of contemporary materialists, not all of whom are dialectical materialists, contributed to the uneven collection of essays edited by Sellars (436).

446 pleads for the objective examination of Marxian theories but makes no genuine philosophical contribution. 451 and 452 are assessments of dialectical materialism by two important American naturalists. Sellars' is the more systematic treatment; Santayana's essay is not on the level of his best work. 462 contains Sartre's most important opinions about the dialectic. In addition to a bibliography of his writings, 470 includes a number of philosophical essays in honor of Lukács' seventieth birthday. 485 distinguishes between "creative" and "dogmatic" Marxism. 480 is a violent attack on Wetter as unscientific and a determined enemy of reason.

414. Acton, H. B. *The Illusion of the Epoch: Marxism-Leninism as a Philosophical Creed.* London: Cohen & West, 1955. 278p.
415. Adoratskii, Vladimir V. *Dialectical Materialism: The Theoretical Foundation of Marxism-Leninism.* New York: International Publishers, 1934. 96p.
416. Bernstein, Samuel, ed. *A Centenary of Marxism.* New York: Science and Society, 1948. 196p.
417. Bukharin, Nikolai I., ed. *Marxism and Modern Thought: A Symposium.* New York: Harcourt, Brace, 1935. 342p.
418. Cohen, Chapman. *Materialism Restated.* London: Pioneer Press, 1943. 210p.
419. Cole, George D. H. *The Meaning of Marxism.* London: Victor Gollancz, 1950. 302p.
420. Conze, Edward. *An Introduction to Dialectical Materialism.* London: N.C.L.C. Publishing Co., 1936. 59p.
421. ———. *The Scientific Method of Thinking.* London: Chapman & Hall, 1935. 168p.
422. Cornforth, Maurice C. *Dialectical Materialism; An Introductory Course.* London: Lawrence & Wishart, 1952.
423. ———. *Philosophy for Socialists.* London: Lawrence & Wishart, 1959. 60p.
424. Eastman, Max. *The Last Stand of Dialectical Materialism.* New York: Polemic Publishers, 1935. 48p.

425. EDWARDS, MALDWYN L., ed. *Communism*. London: Epworth Press, 1952. 64p.

426. HOOK, SIDNEY. *Reason, Social Myths, and Democracy*. New York: John Day, 1940. 302p.

427. HOROWITZ, IRVING L. *Radicalism and the Revolt Against Reason*. New York: Humanities Press, 1961. 264p.

428. INTERNATIONAL CONGRESS OF PHILOSOPHY. *Doklady i vystupleniia predstavitelei sovetskoi filosofskoi nauki na XII mezhdunarodnom filosofskom kongresse*. Moscow: Izdatel'stvo Akademii Nauk, SSSR, 1958. 145p.

429. LA PIRA, GIORGIO, and others. *The Philosophy of Communism*. New York: Fordham University Press, 1952. 308p.

430. LEVY, HERMANN, and others. *Aspects of Dialectical Materialism*. London: Watts, 1934. 154p.

431. McFADDEN, CHARLES J. *The Metaphysical Foundations of Dialectical Materialism*. Washington, D. C.: Catholic University of America, 1938. 206p.

432. ——. *The Philosophy of Communism*. New York: Benziger Bros., 1939. 345p.

433. NOVACK, GEORGE. *The Origins of Materialism*. New York: Merit Publishers, 1965. 300p.

434. ROBERTS, LEO, and CARSON, EDWARD. *Dialectical Materialism: History, Theory and Practice*. New York: International Publishers, 1938.

435. RUDAS, LADISLAUS. *Dialectical Materialism and Communism*. London: Labour Monthly Pamphlets, 1934. 43p.

436. SELLARS, ROY WOOD, ed. *Philosophy for the Future: The Quest of Modern Materialism*. New York: Macmillan, 1949. 675p.

437. THALHEIMER, AUGUST. *Introduction to Dialectical Materialism*. New York: Covici, Friede, 1936. 253p.

438. ACTON, H. B. "The Marxist Outlook," *Philosophy* 22 (1947), 208–30.

439. CARRITT, EDGAR F. "A Discussion of Dialectical Materialism," *The Labour Monthly* 15 (1933), 324–29, 383–91.

440. EASTMAN, MAX. "Against the Marxian Dialectic," *The New Republic* 78 (February 21, 1934), 35–39.

441. FREISTADT, HANS. "Dialectical Materialism: A Friendly Interpretation," *Philosophy of Science* 23 (1956), 97–110.

442. HAY, J. M., and JACKSON, T. A. "A Discussion of Dialectical Materialism," *The Labour Monthly* 15 (1933), 503–11.

443. HOOK, SIDNEY. "The Philosophy of Dialectical Materialism," *Journal of Philosophy* 25 (1928), 113–24, 141–55.

444. ———. "What Is Materialism?" *Journal of Philosophy* 31 (1934), 235–42.

445. KOPNIN, P. V. "Dialectical Materialism and Metaphysics," *International Philosophical Quarterly* 6 (1966), 33–44.

446. LAUER, QUENTIN. "Marxism: Philosophy of Freedom," *Thought* 38 (1963), 22–38.

447. RUDAS, LADISLAUS. "Dialectical Materialism and Communism," *The Labour Monthly* 15 (1933), 568–77, 633–44.

448. ———. "Dialectical Materialism and Communism—A Postscript," *The Labour Monthly* 16 (1934), 563–72.

449. ———. "The Meaning of Sidney Hook," *The Labour Monthly* 17 (1935), 177–84, 249–56, 312–20.

450. SAKSENA, S. K. "Dialectical Materialism," *Philosophy and Phenomenological Research* 10 (1949–50), 541–52.

451. SANTAYANA, GEORGE. "Some Developments of Materialism," *The American Scholar* 18 (1949), 271–81.

452. SELLARS, ROY WOOD. "Reflections on Dialectical Materialism," *Philosophy and Phenomenological Research* 5 (1944–45), 157–79.

453. SIMPSON, HERMAN. "The Marxian Dialectic: A Reply," *The New Republic* 78 (February 28, 1934), 63–67.

454. SLOAN, P. A., THOMAS, L., and LEVY, H. "A Discussion of Dialectical Materialism," *The Labour Monthly* 15 (1933), 441–52.

455. BELLO, C. *Communisme platonicien et marxisme*. Paris: Impressions de Vaugirard, 1950. 252p.

456. BENDA, JULIEN. *Trois idoles romantiques: Le dynamisme, l'existentialisme, la dialectique matérialisme*. Genève: Mont-Blanc, 1948. 175p.

457. GARAUDY, ROGER, et al. *Mésaventures de l'anti-marxisme; les malheurs de M. Merleau-Ponty*. Paris: Éditions sociales, 1956. 159p.

458. GURVITCH, GEORGES. *Dialectique et sociologie*. Paris: Flammarion, 1962. 242p.

459. LEFÈBVRE, HENRI. *Le matérialisme dialectique*. Paris: Presses Universitaires de France, 1947. 153p.

460. NAVILLE, PIERRE. *Psychologie, marxisme, matérialisme*. Paris: M. Rivière. 1946. 206p.

461. POLLÈS, HENRI. *Psychanalyses du communisme*. Paris: H. Lefèbvre, 1949. 568p.

462. SARTRE, JEAN-PAUL. *Critique de la raison dialectique*. Paris: Gallimard, 1960.

463. SOREL, GEORGES. *La décomposition du marxisme*. Paris: M. Rivière, 1910. 68p.

464. ANDREAS, THEODOR. *Zur Widerlegung des dialektischen und historischen Materialismus*. Pfaffenhofen-Lim: Privately printed (?), 1954. 110p.

465. BERLIN. INSTITUT FÜR GESELLSCHAFTSWISSENSCHAFTEN. *Der dialektische Materialismus und der Aufbau des Sozialismus*. Berlin: Dietz, 1958. 190p.

466. BRAUWEILER, HEINZ. *Der dialektische und historische Materialismus*. Berlin: Morus-Verlag, 1950. 46p.

467. BÜTOW, HELLMUTH G. *Die Entwicklung des dialektischen und historischen Materialismus in der Sowjetzone*. Berlin: In Kommission bei Otto Harrassowitz, 1960. Part I, 119p.

468. CVEKL, JUŘI. *Über materialistische Dialektik*. Berlin: Dietz, 1959. 139p.

469. FALK, HEINRICH. *Die ideologischen Grundlagen des Kommunismus*. München: G. Olzog, 1961. 154p.

470. *Georg Lukács zum siebzigsten Geburtstag* (no author). Berlin: Aufbau-Verlag, 1955. 261p.

471. GROPP, RUGARD O. *Der dialektische Materialismus: Kurzer Abriss*. Leipzig: Verlag Enzyklopädie, 1961. 163p.

472. ———. *Was ist dialektische Materialismus?* München: Dobbeck Verlag, 1960. 128p.

473. ———. *Zu Fragen der Geschichte der Philosophie und des dialektischen Materialismus*. Berlin: Deutscher Verlag der Wissenschaften, 1958. 137p.

474. HAFFNER, PAUL L. *Der moderne Materialismus*. St. Louis: F. Saler, 1865. 42p.

475. HAGER, KURT. *Der dialektische Materialismus*. Berlin: Dietz, 1959. 94p.

476. HORZ, H. *Der dialektische Determinismus in Natur und Gesellschaft*. Berlin: Deutscher Verlag der Wissenschaften, 1962. 143p.

477. JANTZEN, NIKOLAI. *Der dialektische Materialismus—der Kompass und Leitfaden im Leben des Menschen*. Berlin: Sozialistische Einheitspartei Deutschlands, 1958. 34p.

478. KARISCH, RUDOLF. *Der dialektische Materialismus: Weltmacht und Weltgefahr*. Leutesdorf am Rhein: Johannes-Verlag, 1956. 32p.

479. KLAUS, GEORG, KOSING, A., und REDLOW, G. *Dialektischer Materialismus*. Berlin: Dietz, 1959. 2 vols.
480. KLAUS, GEORG. *Jesuiten, Gott, Materie*. Berlin: Deutscher Verlag der Wissenschaften, 1958. 360p.
481. LANGE, MAX G. *Marxismus, Leninismus, Stalinismus; Zur Kritik des dialektischen Materialismus*. Stuttgart: Ernst Klett, 1955. 210p.
482. MEHRING, FRANZ. *Philosophische Aufsätze*. Berlin: Dietz, 1961. 486p.
483. OGIERMANN, HELMUT. *Materialistische Dialektik*. München: A. Pustet, 1958. 275p.
484. RUDAS, LADISLAUS. *Der dialektische Materialismus und die Sozialdemokratie*. Moskau-Leningrad: Verlagsgenossenschaft ausländischer Arbeiter in der UdSSR, 1934. 129p.
485. SAUERLAND, KURT. *Die dialektische Materialismus*. Berlin: Universum-Bücherei für Alle, 1932.
486. STEINBERG, HELMUT. *Marxismus, Leninismus, Stalinismus*. Hamburg: Holstein-Verlag, 1955. 101p.
487. STERN, VIKTOR. *Der dialektische Materialismus, die Weltanschauung der marxistisch-leninistischen Partei*. Leipzig: Urania-Verlag, 1954. 35p.
488. ———. *Grundzüge des dialektischen und historischen Materialismus*. Berlin: Dietz, 1947. 87p.
489. WETTER, GUSTAV A. *Ordnung ohne Freiheit; der dialektische Materialismus*. Kevelaer: Butzon & Bercker, 1956. 38p.
490. TROELTSCH, ERNST. "Die marxistische Dialektik" in *Gesammelte Schriften*. Tübingen: Mohr, 1912–25. Vol. III.

See also: 30, 31, 32, 40, 55, 56, 161, 166, 170, 194, 200, 202, 329, 336, 349, 364, 395, 412, 493, 495, 508, 516, 526, 579, 610, 613, 614, 626, 633, 687, 934, 1075, 1101, 1144, 1180, 1182, 1222, 1225, 1231, 1233, 1236, 1239, 1415, 1416, 1464, 1480, 1490, 1505, 1533, 1535, 1539, 1540, 1542, 1548, 1551, 1556.

7 ———————————— THE DIALECTIC

The nature of the dialectic and its laws have not received attention proportionate to their importance. The statements that express the laws have, on the whole, remained imprecise. The "logic" of the laws is inadequately explored. The claims about their applicability and their ontological status are in need of substantiation. While most Marxist-Leninists agree about the importance of developing a dialectical logic, very little of substance has been done to fill this need. Some scholars hope that the relatively recent upsurge of interest in substantive philosophical issues in the Soviet Union and in such countries as Poland and Hungary might yield valuable results in this field. Unfortunately, the reports so far received do not indicate that progress has been spectacular.

An extensive, though often superficial and occasionally incorrect, treatment of the dialectic from the Marxist point of view may be found in 495. 499 is an excellent discussion of the dialectic as a pattern of existential change and as a method of analysis and discovery. 500 is a less convincing study of it in the context of social change and the self-development of man. Part II of 501 contains a naturalistic interpretation of the dialectic with a discussion of the relation of the concept of dialectical development to those of the whole and its parts, time, and change. Popper's account of the central features of the concept of dialectic and of its development from Kant to Marx (502) is vitiated by his apparent inability to forego hasty condemnation.

Among the philosophically more solid treatments of the dialectical method are 493, 508, and 516. 492, 497, and 519 discuss the important issue of objective contradiction. Schaff (503) argues that in speaking of objective contradictions dialectical materialists refer

only to the unity and struggle of opposites; they do not mean to
deny the validity of the logical law of non-contradiction. 513 is a
collection of Soviet texts with commentary on problems relating
to objective contradiction. The treatment of non-antagonistic contradiction in Chapter 5 of 517 is useful and enlightening. 511 presents a discussion of the law of the negation of the negation.

For accounts of dialectical logic the reader may consult 509,
510, and 518, although none of them offers an adequate or even
extensive treatment. 494 has a helpful bibliography of sources in
English and Russian. 491 is useful for comparison with the Marxist-
Leninist view of dialectic. 504 is an elementary explication of the
three laws of the dialectic; the ontological problems announced in
the title are neither identified nor discussed. 505 is an unconvincing
critique of Hook's work on the dialectic.

491. ADLER, MORTIMER J. *Dialectic*. London: Paul, Trench, Trub-
ner, 1927. 265p.
492. CONZE, EDWARD. *Contradiction and Reality*. London: Wight-
man, 1939. 32p.
493. CORNFORTH, MAURICE. *Materialism and the Dialectical Method*. New York: International Publishers, 1960. 141p.
494. FILIPOV, ALEKSANDR P. *Logic and Dialectic in the Soviet
Union*. New York: Research Program on the USSR, 1952.
89p.
495. JACKSON, THOMAS H. *Dialectics*. New York: International
Publishers, 1936. 648p.
496. KIM, CHUN-SŎP. *Dialectical Method*. Ann Arbor, Mich.:
University Microfilms, 1952.
497. MAO, TSE-TUNG. *On Contradiction*. Peking: Foreign Languages Press, 1958. 61p.
498. [not used]

499. HOOK, SIDNEY. "Dialectic in Social and Historical Inquiry,"
Journal of Philosophy 36 (1939), 365–78.
500. ———. "The Marxian Dialectic," *The New Republic* 74
(March 22, 1933), 150–54.
501. ———. "What is Dialectic?" *Journal of Philosophy* 26 (1929),
85–99, 113–23.
502. POPPER, KARL. "What Is Dialectic?" *Mind* 49 (1940), 403–26.
503. SCHAFF, ADAM. "Marxist Dialectics and the Principle of Contradiction," *Journal of Philosophy* 57 (1960), 241–50.

504. SOMERVILLE, JOHN M. "Ontological Problems of Contemporary Dialectical Materialism," *Journal of Philosophy* 35 (1938), 232–36.

505. WILSON, EDMUND. "Taking the Marxist Dialectic Apart," *The New Republic* 91 (1937), 366–68.

506. FOULQUIÉ, PAUL. *La dialectique.* Paris: Presses Universitaires de France, 1949. 127p.

507. LEFÈBVRE, HENRI. *A la lumière du matérialisme dialectique.* Paris: Éditions sociales, 1947.

508. MERLEAU-PONTY, MAURICE. *Les aventures de la dialectique.* Paris: Gallimard, 1955. 313p.

509. FOGARASI, BÉLA. *Logik.* Berlin: Aufbau-Verlag, 1956. 429p.

510. KEDROV, BONIFATII M. *Die dialektische Logik und die Naturwissenschaft.* Leipzig: Verlag Enzyklopädie, 1960. 18p.

511. ———. *Gibt es eine Höherentwicklung?* Leipzig: Urania-Verlag, 1959. 121p.

512. KOZLOVSKII, V. *Antagonistische und nichtantagonistische Widersprüche.* Berlin: Dietz, 1956. 95p.

513. LOBKOWICZ, NIKOLAUS. *Das Widerspruchsprinzip in der neueren sowjetischen Philosophie.* Dordrecht, Holland: D. Reidel, 1960. 90p.

514. MARCK, SIEGFRIED. *Die Dialektik in der Philosophie der Gegenwart.* Tübingen: Mohr, 1929–31.

515. ROZENTAL, MARK M. *Die Dialektik in Marx' Kapital.* Berlin: Dietz, 1957. 446p.

516. ———. *Die marxistische dialektische Methode.* Berlin: Dietz, 1953. 352p.

517. STIEHLER, GOTTFRIED. *Hegel und der Marxismus über den Widerspruch.* Berlin: Dietz, 1960. 206p.

518. *Über formale Logik und Dialektik.* Diskussions-Beiträge. Kosing, A. und Kosing, E., eds. Berlin: Verlag Kultur und Fortschritt, 1952. 216p.

519. VETTER, HERMANN. *Die Stellung des dialektischen Materialismus zum Prinzip des ausgeschlossenen Widerspruchs.* Berlin: Der Meiler, 1962. 84p.

520. WENZL, ALOYS. *Bedeutung und Vieldeutigkeit der Dialektik.* München: Verlag der Bayerischen Akademie der Wissenschaften, 1959. 17p.

See also: 31, 398, 407, 426, 430, 448, 453, 459, 468, 483, 490, 552, 613, 631, 633, 668, 718, 736, 972.

8 – DIALECTICAL MATERIALISM, SCIENCE, AND THE SCIENTIFIC METHOD

Discussions of the relation of dialectical materialism to science and the scientific method suffer from two major weaknesses. The first is the excessive and unsupportable claims Marxists tend to make for the relevance, even indispensability, of their principles to scientific investigation. A good example of such exaggerated contentions is 557, which argues that the principles of dialectics and of philosophical materialism form the foundation of the theory and practice of physicists everywhere. Another example is 561, which bills the theory of relativity as a "brilliant confirmation" of the truth of dialectical materialism. 534 is a panegyric on the unlimited usefulness of Marxism-Leninism for the physical and social sciences.

The second weakness is the relative ignorance of the philosophy of science, which the work of many dialectical materialists reveals. A good example of such philosophical unsophistication is 549, in which the author shows himself unaware of most of the developments in the philosophy of science relevant to his topic which have occurred since Kant. Another example is 551, which extols the importance of Leninist materialism for twentieth-century developments in physics. 548 does not quite manage to draw the distinction between the theories of science and the theorizing of scientists: it is dubious that the author of 553 has any clear notion of the nature of scientific hypotheses or of the epistemological problems connected with their confirmation.

Despite these weaknesses, some good work has been done in the field. 524 is an attempt by a British scientist to give a Marxist-Leninist account of the relations of science to the social and economic conditions of society. 579 is an insightful treatment of Marx's view of nature. Hook's discussion of dialectical materialism and the scientific method (535) is based on Chapter 9 of 426; it is the best single discussion of the topic, even though it is far from exhaustive and suffers from some hasty judgments. 577 contains a useful discussion of problems relating to the nature of matter. 526 and 550 include work on the scientific method and on such central concepts as that of causation.

For general discussions of the relation of dialectical materialism to science the reader may consult 537, 564, 572, 576, and 583 with profit. Other general examinations are 539, 545, 556, 571, and 575, but they are of very limited value. 546 and 581 deal with physics; 563 gives an account of the influence of Marxist-Leninist philosophy on the theories of Soviet scientists concerning the nature and origin of the universe. 578 is an impressive review of philosophical disagreements about the theory of relativity between Soviet philosophers and physicists.

580 is the best work available on the dialectical materialist philosophy of biology, even though the book leaves much unresolved. 538 gives the Marxist view of evolution and Social Darwinism with a minimum of sophistication. In 555 the specific relation between "Bolshevik principles" and Russian physiology remains unexplored to the end. The relation of Marx and Freud is the subject under study in 521, 541, and 543. 568 finds some interesting parallels between Marx's social theory and Freud's psychology; 533 gives the unique mixture of Freud and Marx which we have come to associate with Fromm's work.

570 argues that the Marxist view of history is not scientific and that Marx had at best an inadequate notion of the nature of physical science. The latter claim receives indirect support from 562, in which the view is set forth that Marxism is a theory about the development of human society: it has nothing to do with physical science or with theories about the ultimate nature of the universe. One of 560's hazy theses is that Marx's great contribution to history was the expression and resolution of "the fundamental antinomies of human life."

522 is a collection of essays on topics ranging from the social function of science to the Marxist-Leninist philosophy of science. 527 incorporates two of Cornforth's earlier books: *In Defense of Philosophy* and *Science and Idealism*. It is a Marxist defense of philosophy against logical positivist and pragmatist attacks. 529 and 566 are polemical pieces. 530 is a study of Darwin, Spencer, and Marx. Feuer argues (552) that if the laws of the dialectic are taken as the suggested forms of scientific laws, then they may prove useful but are by no means obviously true. If, however, they are accepted as dogmatically true, then they tend to inhibit the development of science. 554 is an unsystematic exploration of why Marxism is attractive to some scientists. 565 is an imprecise contrast of the inflexibility of orthodox Marxism-Leninism with the rationality of an enlightened naturalist philosophy of science. 567 expounds the interesting view that the laws of the dialectic are empirical generalizations, but leaves it, unfortunately, without adequate support.

Special mention should be given to the Joint Publications Research Service for their useful program of translations. Their 540, 542, and 547 are valuable sources of information to the researcher. 536 is a collection of papers read by Soviet philosophers at the Thirteenth International Congress of Philosophy.

521. BARTLETT, FRANCIS H. *Sigmund Freud: A Marxian Essay*. London: V. Gollancz, 1938. 141p.
522. BERNAL, JOHN D. *The Freedom of Necessity*. London: Routledge and Kegan Paul, 1949. 437p.
523. ———. *Marx and Science*. New York: International Publishers, 1952. 48p.
524. ———. *The Social Function of Science*. London: Routledge, 1939. 482p.
525. BUKHARIN, NIKOLAI I., and others. *Marxism and Modern Thought*. London: Routledge, 1935. 342p.
526. CORNFORTH, MAURICE C. *Dialectical Materialism and Science*. London: Lawrence & Wishart, 1949. 63p.
527. ———. *Science versus Idealism*. New York: International Publishers, 1962. 464p.
528. DUCLOS, JACQUES. *Communism, Science and Culture*. New York: International Publishers, 1939. 46p.

529. EASTMAN, MAX. *Marxism, Is It Science?* New York: Norton, 1940. 394p.

530. FERRI, E. *Socialism and Modern Science.* New York: International Library, 1900. 213p.

531. FISCHER, GEORGE. *Science and Politics: The New Sociology in the Soviet Union.* Ithaca, N.Y.: Cornell University Press, 1964. 66p.

532. FOK, VLADIMIR. *The Theory of Space, Time and Gravitation.* New York: Pergamon Press, 1959. 411p.

533. FROMM, ERICH. *Beyond the Chains of Illusion.* New York: Simon and Schuster, 1962. 182p.

534. HALDANE, JOHN B. S. *The Marxist Philosophy and the Sciences.* New York: Random House, 1939. 214p.

535. HOOK, SIDNEY. *Dialectical Materialism and Scientific Method.* Manchester, England: Bulletin of the Committee on Science and Freedom, 1955. 32p.

536. INTERNATIONAL CONGRESS OF PHILOSOPHY. *Philosophy, Science and Man.* Moscow: Academy of Sciences of the USSR, 1963. 174p.

537. LEVY, HYMAN. *Modern Science.* New York: Knopf, 1939. 736p.

538. LEWIS, JOHN. *Man and Evolution.* New York: International Publishers, 1962. 150p.

539. LINDSAY, JACK. *Marxism and Contemporary Science.* London: D. Dobson, 1949. 261p.

540. MOROZOV, K. Y. *Philosophical Questions of Mathematics.* Washington, D.C.: Joint Publications Research Service, 1964. 46p.

541. OSBERT, REUBEN. (OSBORN, R., pseud.). *Freud and Marx. A Dialectical Study.* London: V. Gollancz, 1937. 285p.

542. *Philosophical Problems in Sociology and Natural Science: USSR* (no author). Washington, D.C.: Joint Publications Research Service, 1964. 51p.

543. SCHANCK, RICHARD L. *The Permanent Revolution in Science.* New York: Philosophical Library, 1954. 112p.

544. *Science at the Crossroads.* Papers presented to the International Congress of the History of Science and Technology ... by delegates of the USSR. London: Kniga, Ltd., 1931. 233p.

545. SPRATT, PHILIP. *Diamat as Philosophy of Nature.* Bombay: Libertarian Social Institute, 1958. 122p.

546. SPRIGG, CHRISTOPHER S. (CAUDWELL, CHRISTOPHER, pseud.). *The Crisis in Physics.* London: John Lane, 1939. 245p.

547. VIGDOROVICH, M. I., ed. *Dialectical Materialism and Present-Day Natural Science*. Washington, D.C.: Joint Publications Research Service, Office of Technical Services, U.S. Department of Commerce, 1965. 379p.

548. BERNAL, JOHN D. "Engels and Science," *The Labour Monthly* 17 (1935), 506–13.

549. DUTT, CLEMENS. "Dialectical Materialism and Natural Science; Rejoinder," *The Labour Monthly* 15 (1933), 84–95.

550. EMERY, A. "Dialectics versus Mechanics," *Philosophy of Science* 2 (1935), 9–38.

551. EPSTEIN, PAUL S. "The Diamat and Modern Science," *Bulletin of the Atomic Scientists* 8 (1952), 190–94.

552. FEUER, LEWIS S. "Dialectical Materialism and Soviet Science," *Philosophy of Science* 16 (1949), 105–24.

553. FREISTADT, HANS. "Dialectical Materialism: A Further Discussion," *Philosophy of Science* 24 (1957), 25–49.

554. FRIEWALD, E. M. "Marxism and Science," *Spectator* 183 (1949), 136–37.

555. GANTT, W. HORSLEY. "Bolshevik Principles and Russian Physiology," *Bulletin of the Atomic Scientists* 8 (1952), 183–89.

556. HALDANE, JOHN B. S. "Dialectical Materialism and Modern Science," *The Labour Monthly* 23 (1941), 266–68, 327–30, 400–2, 430–32.

557. HOLLITSCHER, WALTER. "Dialectical Materialism and the Physicist," *Bulletin of the Atomic Scientists* 9 (1953), 54–57.

558. HOOK, SIDNEY. "Marx and Darwinism," *The New Republic* 67 (1931), 290.

559. ———. "Marx and Freud: Oil and Water," *Open Court* 42 (1928), 20–25.

560. KRIEGER, LEONARD. "Uses of Marx for History," *Political Science Quarterly* 75 (1960), 355–78.

561. LENZ, J. "Einstein and Dialectical Materialism," *The Labour Monthly* 2 (1929), 220–23.

562. MATTICK, PAUL. "Marxism and the New Physics," *Philosophy of Science* 29 (1962), 350–64.

563. MIKULAK, MAXIM W. "Soviet Philosophic-Cosmological Thought," *Philosophy of Science* 25 (1958), 35–50.

564. "Philosophy and the Natural Sciences in the USSR" (report

of a conference on the philosophical problems of science, Moscow, 1958), *Daedelus* 89 (1960), 632–47.

565. RIEPE, DALE. "Flexible Scientific Naturalism and Dialectical Fundamentalism," *Philosophy of Science* 25 (1958), 241–48.

566. SOMERVILLE, JOHN. "Open Letter to Bertrand Russell," *Philosophy of Science* 13 (1946), 67–71.

567. ——. "Soviet Science and Dialectical Materialism," *Philosophy of Science* 12 (1945), 23–29.

568. SOULE, GEORGE. "Psychology and Revolution," *The New Republic* 92 (August 25, 1937), 66–72.

569. WETTER, GUSTAV A. "Ideology and Science in the Soviet Union: Recent Developments," *Daedalus* 89 (1960), 581–603.

570. WOOD, H. G. "Marx and Science," *Hibbert Journal* 54 (1956), 226–34.

571. BERLIN. INSTITUT FÜR GESELLSCHAFTSWISSENSCHAFTEN. *Naturwissenschaft und Philosophie.* Leipzig: Urania-Verlag, 1959. 81p.

572. HOLLITSCHER, WALTER. *Die Natur im Weltbild der Wissenschaft.* Wien: Globus Verlag, 1960. 499p.

573. KLAUS, GEORG. *Kybernetik in philosophischer Sicht.* Berlin: Dietz, 1961. 491p.

574. ——. *Philosophie und Einzelwissenschaft.* Berlin: Deutscher Verlag der Wissenschaften, 1958. 73p.

575. KUCZYNSKI, JÜRGEN. *Fortschrittliche Wissenschaft.* Berlin: Aufbau-Verlag, 1951. 165p.

576. *Marxismus und Naturwissenschaft.* Intro. by Otto Jenssen. Berlin: E. Laub, 1925. 180p.

577. MEUERS, JOSEPH. *Wissenschaft im Kollektiv.* München: A. Pustet, 1959. 231p.

578. MÜLLER-MARKUS, SIEGFRIED. *Einstein und die Sowjetphilosophie.* Dordrecht, Holland: D. Reidel, 1960–66. Vol. I: 481p. Vol. II: 510p.

579. SCHMIDT, ALFRED. *Der Begriff der Natur in der Lehre von Marx.* Frankfurt am Main: Europäische Verlagsanstalt, 1962. 182p.

580. SEGAL, JACOB. *Die dialektische Methode in der Biologie.* Berlin: Dietz, 1958. 271p.

581. STERN, VIKTOR. *Raum, Zeit, Bewegung im Lichte der modernen Naturwissenschaft.* Berlin: Aufbau-Verlag, 1955. 104p.

582. WETTER, GUSTAV A. *Der dialektische Materialismus und das Problem der Entstehung des Lebens.* München-Salzburg-Köln: Anton Pustet, 1958. 71p.

583. ——. *Philosophie und Naturwissenschaft in der Sowjetunion.* Hamburg: Rowholt, 1958. 195p.

584. ZWEILING, KLAUS. *Der Leninsche Materiebegriff und seine Bestätigung durch die moderne Atomphysik.* Berlin: Dietz, 1956. 63p.

See also: 28, 30, 31, 40, 58, 200, 334, 367, 396, 417, 419, 421, 426, 476, 510, 598, 599, 617, 630, 634, 688, 690, 694, 719, 912, 921, 954, 959, 1151, 1184, 1239, 1253, 1332, 1335, 1339, 1341, 1344, 1345, 1346, 1348, 1349, 1354, 1362, 1365, 1367, 1369, 1490, 1492.

9 — DIALECTICAL MATERIALISM AND PSYCHOLOGY

Psychology, philosophical psychology, and the philosophy of psychology are of special importance for the insight they can afford into the nature of man. Unfortunately, relatively little has been done to develop the philosophical psychology implicit in dialectical materialism; equally little effort has been made to deal with the philosophical problems peculiar to a psychology that is materialistic in orientation but wishes to avoid the excesses of behaviorism. The theoretical essays of a number of Soviet psychologists, however, have been translated, and it is to them that we must turn for most of the enlightenment that may be had concerning the Marxist-Leninist science of man.

588 is a good history of alterations and developments in Soviet psychology. The author attempts to view the changing Soviet

conception of man as a reflection of "changing ideological, political, and practical pressures." 591 contains materials on the Marxist interpretation of literature and morals, in addition to psychology. 597 is a collection of papers by Russian scientists. The topics discussed include the general orientation of Soviet psychology and some problems of educational psychology.

598 and 599 are interesting samples of the work of a leading American dialectical materialist. 598 is the more convincing of the two books, although even it lacks the philosophical caution requisite in a field that abounds in pitfalls. 600 is another collection of translated essays. 602 is a weak attack on Freud; 605 is a brief review of the recent history of Soviet psychology and psychiatry. 603 gives an account of Soviet attacks on psychology for dealing with the "abstract human personality," instead of the concrete, socially conditioned individual. 606 is a sketch of the aims, views, and methods of Soviet psychology as gleaned in a six-week visit to the USSR.

The person interested in tracing the important influence of Pavlov on Soviet psychology had best begin with Pavlov's famous 592; 593 and 594 are good collections of Pavlov's work. 585 is the stenographic account of the scientific meeting that established the "official" direction of Soviet psychology. 589 and 590 are standard textbooks; a number of other texts are also available through the English language editions of Foreign Languages Publishing House. 586 is a simple, though interesting, account of some of the implications of Pavlov's work and thought.

585. AKADEMIIA NAUK SSSR. *Scientific Session on the Physiological Teachings of Academician I. P. Pavlov.* Moscow: Foreign Languages Publishing House, 1951. 173p.
586. ASRATIAN, EZRAS A. *I. P. Pavlov: His Life and Work.* Moscow: Foreign Languages Publishing House, 1953. 163p.
587. BARAN, PAUL A. *Marxism and Psychoanalysis.* New York: Monthly Review Press, 1960. 64p.
588. BAUER, RAYMOND A. *The New Man in Soviet Psychology.* Cambridge, Mass.: Harvard University Press, 1952. 229p.
589. BYKOV, KONSTANTIN M. *Textbook of Physiology.* Moscow: Foreign Languages Publishing House, 1958. 762p.
590. IVANOV-SMOLENSKII, A. G. *Essays on the Patho-Physiology of the Higher Nervous Activity According to I. P. Pavlov*

and his School. Moscow: Foreign Languages Publishing House, 1954. 348p.

591. LEWIS, C. DAY, ed. *The Mind in Chains; Socialism and the Cultural Revolution*. London: F. Muller, 1937. 255p.

592. PAVLOV, IVAN P. *Conditioned Reflexes*. New York: Dover, 1960. 430p.

593. ———. *Experimental Psychology and Other Essays*. New York: Philosophical Library, 1957. 653p.

594. ———. *Selected Works*. Moscow: Foreign Languages Publishing House, 1955. 661p.

595. SECHENOV, IVAN M. *Selected Physiological and Psychological Works*. New York: Universal Distributors, 1962. 607p.

596. SIMON, BRIAN, ed. *Psychology in the Soviet Union*. Stanford, Calif.: Stanford University Press, 1957. 305p.

597. *Soviet Psychology: A Symposium*. New York: Philosophical Library, 1961. 109p.

598. WELLS, HARRY K. *Ivan P. Pavlov: Toward a Scientific Psychology and Psychiatry*. New York: International Publishers, 1956. 224p.

599. ———. *Sigmund Freud: A Pavlovian Critique*. New York: International Publishers, 1960. 252p.

600. WINN, RALPH B., ed. *Psychotherapy in the Soviet Union*. New York: Philosophical Library, 1961. 207p.

601. WORTIS, JOSEPH. *Soviet Psychiatry*. Baltimore: Williams and Wilkins, 1950. 314p.

602. BERNAL, J. D. "Psycho-Analysis and Marxism," *The Labour Monthly* 19 (1937), 433–37.

603. DAVIES, R. G. "Mind of Man: Soviet View; Normal and Abnormal in the USSR," *Commentary* 11 (1951), 488–94.

604. KNOBLACH, FERDINAND. "Marxists Reject Libido Theory," *International Journal of Psychiatry* 2 (1966), 558–60.

605. LONDON, IVAN D. "Soviet Psychology and Psychiatry," *Bulletin of the Atomic Scientists* 8 (1952), 70–73.

606. RAZRAN, GREGORY H. S. "Psychology in the USSR," *Journal of Philosophy* 32 (1935), 19–24.

607. HALFTER, MAGDALENA. *Der anthropologische Aspekt in der marxistischen Psychologie*. München: Privately printed, 1957. 155p.

See also: 227, 521, 533, 541, 543, 559, 568, 1193, 1194, 1330, 1340, 1350, 1355, 1360.

IO ——————— EPISTEMOLOGY AND
THE PHILOSOPHY OF MIND

German scholars have taken the lead in discussions of the epistemology of dialectical materialism. 617 is a good example of valuable recent work in this field. Horn's treatment of the theory of reflection (626) is the best in a much-neglected field. 619, 624, and 625 are also noteworthy, albeit inadequately developed, contributions to the literature. The best readily available English study is 610. The value of 609 derives from the information it provides on developments in Soviet epistemology; unfortunately, this reporting function makes it impossible for the book to present a full philosophical analysis. Garaudy's work (614) contains some original material; it is the best treatment available in French.

632 and 636 are relatively popular outlines. Both 629 and 634 may be consulted with profit. Schaff's book (633) is an important one on problems relating to the dialectical materialist conception of truth. The author is among the small number of Marxist-Leninists whose work has benefited from a careful study of analytical philosophy.

The nature of consciousness is discussed in 620, 624, and 626; the related problem of the nature of matter is explored in some detail in 630, 635, 637, and 622. The last of these is a group of translations from the 1954 edition of the Soviet Encyclopedia. The problems of a materialist philosophy of mind come to a head in an interesting though inconclusive discussion in 628. A systematic and solidly developed treatment of the categories of dialectical materialism may be found in 631. 616 is a look at Soviet studies in ontology since the death of Stalin. 608 includes essays by Hungarian Marxist-Leninists on such topics as purposiveness, causality, and contradiction. Lewis (611) attacks various forms of "idealism" in recent philosophy. He is certain that dialectical materialism provides the only sound epistemology today; the reader who wishes to see such opinions substantiated will not be equally convinced.

The serious student cannot fail to register general disappointment that so many of the important traditional problems of epistemology have, to date, received inadequate attention from Marxist-Leninists. The last (and perhaps the first) major dialectical materialist work on the theory of perception was Lenin's *Materialism and Empirio-Criticism*, and even that raised more issues than it resolved. Problems relating to induction and the justification of belief, to *a priori* knowledge and the role of universals in cognition remain virtually untouched in any of the three languages of this bibliography. Perhaps dialectical materialism can make no significant contributions to the resolution of such issues. I am certain that Marxist-Leninists will deny this vigorously; but if they do, it is up to them to show what form these contributions will take. Whatever valid insights they can add to current discussions will profit philosophers of all persuasions alike.

608. ACADEMIAE SCIENTIARUM HUNGARICAE. *Studia Philosophica*. Vol. 3: Varia. Budapest: Publishing House of the Hungarian Academy of Science, 1963. 495p.
609. BLAKELEY, THOMAS J. *Soviet Theory of Knowledge*. Dordrecht, Holland: D. Reidel, 1964. 203p.
610. CORNFORTH, MAURICE. *The Theory of Knowledge*. New York: International Publishers, 1955. 240p.
611. LEWIS, JOHN. *Marxism and the Irrationalists*. London: Lawrence & Wishart, 1955. 141p.

612. DUNHAM, BARROWS. "On Teaching Marxist Epistemology," *Philosophy of Science* 19 (1962), 365–68.
613. SHUR, E. "The Theory of the Concept, the Judgment, and the Inference in Formal and Dialectic Logic," *Philosophy and Phenomenological Research* 5 (1944–45), 199–216.

614. GARAUDY, ROGER. *La theorie matérialiste de la connaissance*. Paris: Presses Universitaires de France, 1953. 387p.

615. MOLLE, GERMAINE VAN. *La connaissance dialectique et l'expérience existentielle.* Paris: J. Vrin, 1945. 174p.
616. PLANTY-BONJOUR, GUY. *Les categories du materialisme dialectique.* Dordrecht, Holland: D. Reidel, 1965. 206p.

617. ALBRECHT, ERHARD. *Beiträge zur Erkenntnistheorie und das Verhältnis von Sprache und Denken.* Halle: M. Niemeyer, 1959. 570p.
618. ——. *Das nichtmarxistische Denken in seinem Verhältnis zur Erkennbarkeit der Welt.* Rostock, 1949 (?). 39p.
619. BAUMGARTEN, ARTHUR. *Bemerkungen zur Erkenntnistheorie des dialektischen und historischen Materialismus.* Berlin: Akademie-Verlag, 1957. 181p.
620. BELOV, P. T. *Über den primären Charakter der Materie und den sekundären Charakter des Bewusstseins.* Berlin: Dietz, 1955. 74p.
621. BERLIN, INSTITUT FÜR GESELLSCHAFTSWISSENSCHAFTEN. *Zur aktuellen Bedeutung von Lenins Werk "Materialismus und Empiriokritizismus."* Berlin: Dietz, 1960. 171p.
622. BOL'SHAIA SOVIETSKAIA ENTSIKLOPEDIIA. *Die Materie. Der Materialismus. Materialismus und Empirio-Kritizismus.* Berlin: Dietz, 1956. 64p.
623. FOGARASI, BÉLA. *Kritik des physikalischen Idealismus.* Berlin: Aufbau-Verlag, 1953. 114p.
624. GROPP, RUGARD O. *Die Grundfrage der Philosophie; die Entstehung und Bedeutung des Denkens.* Leipzig: Verlag Enzyklopädie, 1958. 27p.
625. ——. *Über Kausalität, Notwendigkeit und Zufälligkeit.* Leipzig: Verlag Enzyklopädie, 1959. 18p.
626. HORN, JOHANNES H. *Widerspiegelung und Begriff.* Berlin: Deutsche Verlag der Wissenschaften, 1958. 246p.
627. KEDROV, BONIFATII M. *Über Inhalt und Umfang eines sich verändernden Begriff.* Berlin: Deutscher Verlag der Wissenschaften, 1956. 102p.
628. KHASKHACHIKH, F. I. *Materie und Bewusstsein.* Berlin. Dietz, 1955. 227p.
629. MEUSEL, ALFRED. *Untersuchungen über das Erkenntnisobjekt bei Marx.* Jena: G. Fischer, 1925. 105p.
630. OVCHINNIKOV, N. F. *Der Materialität der Welt und die Gesetzmässigkeiten der Entwicklung der sich bewegenden Materie.* Berlin: Dietz, 1954. 56p.

631. ROSENTHAL, MARK M. *Kategorien der materialistischen Dialektik.* Berlin: Dietz, 1959. 430p.
632. ——. *Was ist marxistische Erkenntnistheorie?* Berlin: Dietz, 1956. 76p.
633. SCHAFF, ADAM. *Zu einigen Fragen der marxistischen Theorie der Wahrheit.* Berlin: Dietz, 1954. 507p.
634. STERN, VIKTOR. *Erkenntnistheoretische Probleme der modernen Physik.* Berlin: Aufbau-Verlag, 1952. 104p.
635. ——. *Zu einigen Fragen der marxistischen Philosophie.* Berlin: Aufbau-Verlag, 1954. 119p.
636. VRIES, JOSEF DE. *Die Erkenntnistheorie des dialektischen Materialismus.* München: A. Pustet, 1958. 188p.
637. WENZL, ALOYS. *Der Begriff der Materie und das Problem des Materialismus.* München: Verlag der Bayerischen Akademie der Wissenschaften, 1958. 13p.

See also: 30, 31, 32, 40, 414, 432, 443, 492, 527, 540, 546, 549, 552, 564, 577, 912, 924, 1199, 1372, 1490.

II — HISTORICAL MATERIALISM

Historical materialism is the most thoroughly explored topic in the philosophy of Marxism-Leninism. At least a part of the reason for this is that the interpretation of history is indubitably at the heart of Marxist thought. The philosophy of history is the field in which Marxism-Leninism made its most original theoretical contributions; it has also served as the groundwork of Marxist revolutionary practice. Although there is no final adequate assessment of the validity of historical materialism, a substantial amount of the analytic work necessary for this has already been performed. In what follows I shall call attention to the books that contain the most successful analyses. Virtually all the works listed here contain discussions of one or another set of theories subsidiary to historical materialism. For this reason, it is probable that the person who wishes to examine such topics as the class struggle, the nature of revolution, and the relation of the economic substructure to the ideological superstructure will sooner or later be led to books listed in this general section. In order to identify the relevant books, the reader should consult the "See also" rubric of the section that deals with the field of his specific interest.

Among the creative elaborations of the principles of historical materialism 656 and 664 demand special attention. 736 is an important study of problems relating to the dialectical interpretation of history by the most outstanding Marxist-Leninist philosopher alive. 717 and 729 are major studies by men sympathetic to the view; 644 is a readable exposition and defense by a British Marxist. Other major studies are 706, 723, and 748. 639 is a full, though not outstanding examination: it places special emphasis on the presuppositions of the materialistic conception of history about the nature of man. 641 examines how belief in inevitable historical development may be reconciled with the call for participation in revolutionary activity. 665 criticizes simple economic determinism. 670 is a fresh and insightful examination of the precursors and followers, strengths and weaknesses of Marx's view of history.

Among general introductions to historical materialism 681 and 693 are the briefest and most readable. Other introductory works of some value are 648, 649, 659, 720, and 745. The most substantial elementary discussion by a historical materialist is 642. 724, 725, and 732 are designed to convince those with no background in philosophy. In 704 Wilson argues that Marxism is a scientific view of society and culture. By contrast, 682 contends that there is at most a grain of truth in historical materialism; 698 lists an inadequate theory of classes and dogmatism in method as two of the main causes of its alleged failure.

Other introductory critiques include 653 and 701. In the latter Russell details the inadequacies of the Marxist view of history, of the class struggle, and of the second stage of communism. In the third part of the article he presents his own alternative to Marxism. 690 argues that the theory of the dialectical development of history cannot be both a scientific law and also universal and necessary. 694 is a weak attempt to show that it fails all the tests of a scientific theory; 669 maintains that it is an inadequately substantiated *a priori* conception. Among the poorest elementary treatments is 697, which claims that the only test of historical knowledge is sound political action. 679 informs us in a disarmingly simple way that Marx is wrong because real history is the sacramental history of God's actions in the world. Daniels' 680 about Marx's and Stalin's views of historical necessity is a remarkable collection of conceptual muddles.

645, 666, 673, 674, 714, 726, 730, 743, and 746 contain critical evaluations of historical materialism. 645 is by a leading idealist philosopher; on the whole, however, Turgeon's analyses (714) are more detailed and more incisive. 666 is an impassioned attack on "historicism" from Plato to Marx, providing the sort of withering skeptical look at theories about large-scale historical trends which, even if it fails to convince, helps to clarify the issues involved. William's (673) contrast between consumer-oriented and producer-oriented political systems is promising, but he appears unable to do anything with it. His work suffers, as does 674, from occasional vagueness, overstatement, and bombast. 674 attacks theories maintaining that human society undergoes a unilinear historical development on the basis of an interesting analysis of the tradition of Asiatic despotism. 726, 743, and 746 include substantial expositions as well as critical remarks.

640 contains a non-technical exposition of historical materialism. Boudin attempts to view Marx's social and economic theories as constituting a unified system. 650 is a group of selections from the work of a well-known Italian Marxist. 651 and 709 are mainly of historical interest: the author was a leading French socialist around the turn of the century. 658 is by another leading Marxist of the same period; Luxemburg's work, however, is of continuing theoretical interest. Liebknecht (735) is an enthusiastic revolutionary; Mehring (740) shows himself to be a man of greater refinement, though not of inferior intellect or insight. 654 is a Marxist-Leninist critique of Toynbee's work. 668 claims that the Marxist analysis of social development is of continuing relevance and contains significant discussions of such central concepts as those of class, dialectic, and the Communist society of the future. 678 and 691 agree that Marx was probably right in his claim that

historical trends are determined by economic and social forces rather than by individuals or ideals. 691 adds, however, that in the immediate choice of action the individual and his convictions play an important role. 677 contains remarks by a leading American philosopher about historical materialism. 676 is a Yugoslav Marxist's response to Blanshard.

689 is an able and informative look at Mondolfo's inadequately known book (711). 700 discusses Marx's view of the role of heroes and classes in the plot of history in terms borrowed from drama. Chapter 10 of 708 is an account of the sociological views of the young Marx. 718 and 744 contain contributions to the materialist conception of history and to the notion of dialectical development. Although historical materialism is not the main topic of 643, 646, 647, and 663, they include brief discussions of it and of some related issues.

638. BERLIN, ISAIAH. *Historical Inevitability*. New York: Oxford University Press, 1955. 79p.

639. BOBER, MANDELL M. *Karl Marx's Interpretation of History*. Cambridge, Mass.: Harvard University Press, 1948. 445p.

640. BOUDIN, LOUIS B. *The Theoretical System of Karl Marx in the Light of Recent Criticism*. Chicago: C. H. Kerr, 1907. 286p.

641. BRAMELD, THEODORE B. H. *A Philosophic Approach to Communism*. Chicago: University of Chicago Press, 1933. 235p.

642. BUKHARIN, NIKOLAI I. *Historical Materialism; a System of Sociology*. New York: International Publishers, 1925. 318p.

643. BUTTERFIELD, HERBERT. *History and Human Relations*. New York: Macmillan, 1952. 254p.

644. CORNFORTH, MAURICE. *Historical Materialism*. New York: International Publishers, 1954. 206p.

645. CROCE, BENEDETTO. *Historical Materialism and the Economics of Karl Marx*. New York: Macmillan, 1914. 188p.

646. DIAMOND, STANLEY, ed. *Culture in History*. New York: Columbia University Press, 1960. 1014p.

647. DOBB, MAURICE H. *On Economic Theory and Socialism*. New York: International Publishers, 1955. 293p.

648. FEDERN, KARL. *The Materialist Conception of History*. London: Macmillan, 1939. 262p.

649. GLEZERMAN, G. *The Laws of Social Development*. Moscow: Foreign Languages Publishing House, n.d. 278p.

650. GRAMSCI, ANTONIO. *The Modern Prince, and Other Writings*. London: Lawrence & Wishart, 1957. 192p.

651. JAURÈS, JEAN LÉON. *Studies in Socialism*. New York: Putnam, 1906. 197p.

652. KAUTSKY, KARL. *The Economic Doctrines of Karl Marx*. London: A. C. Black, 1925. 248p.

653. KELSEN, HANS. *The Political Theory of Bolshevism*. Berkeley: University of California Press, 1948. 60p.

654. KOMINSKII, Y. *Professor Toynbee's Philosophy of History*. Moscow: Progress Publishers, 1965. 71p.

655. KONSTANTINOV, F., and KELLE, V. *Historical Materialism: The Marxist Sociology*. Moscow: Novosti Press Agency Publishing House, 1966. 40p.

656. LABRIOLA, ANTONIO. *Essays on the Materialistic Conception of History*. Chicago: C. H. Kerr, 1904. 246p.

657. LEVY, HYMAN. *Social Thinking*. London: Cobbett Press, 1945. 174p.

658. LUXEMBURG, ROSA. *The Russian Revolution* and *Leninism or Marxism?* Ann Arbor, Mich.: University of Michigan Press, 1961. 116p.

659. MEHNERT, KLAUS. *Stalin versus Marx: The Stalinist Historical Doctrine*. London: Allen & Unwin, 1952. 127p.

660. MEYER, ALFRED G. *Leninism*. Cambridge, Mass.: Harvard University Press, 1957. 324p.

661. MOORE, STANLEY W. *Three Tactics: The Background in Marx*. New York: The Monthly Review Press, 1963. 96p.

662. PARCE, LIDA. *Economic Determinism*. Chicago: Kerr, 1913. 155p.

663. PARSONS, TALCOTT. *Essays in Sociological Theory*. Glencoe, Ill.: Free Press, 1949. 366p.

664. PLEKHANOV, GEORGII V. *In Defense of Materialism: The Development of the Monist View of History*. London: Lawrence & Wishart, 1947. 303p.

665. ———. *The Materialist Conception of History*. New York: International Publishers, 1940. 48p.

666. POPPER, KARL R. *The Open Society and Its Enemies*. Princeton: Princeton University Press, 1950. 732p.

667. PRITCHARD, EDGAR W. *The New Dialectics and Social Reform*. Marryatville, S. Australia: Privately printed (?), 1950. 18p.

668. SCHLESINGER, RUDOLF. *Marx: His Time and Ours.* New York: Augustus M. Kelley, 1950. 440p.
669. SÉE, HENRI EUGENE. *The Economic Interpretation of History.* New York: Adelphi Co., 1929. 154p.
670. SELIGMAN, EDWIN R. A. *The Economic Interpretation of History.* New York: Columbia University Press, 1924. 166p.
671. SHAKHNAZAROV, GEORGII. *Man, Science and Society.* Moscow: Progress Publishers, 1965. 314p.
672. SOMERVILLE, JOHN M. *Methodology in Social Science; A Critique of Marx and Engels.* New York: Privately printed, 1938. 72p.
673. WILLIAM, MAURICE. *The Social Interpretation of History.* New York: Sotery Publishing Co., 1921. 397p.
674. WITTFOGEL, KARL A. *Oriental Despotism.* New Haven: Yale University Press, 1957. 556p.
675. WITT-HANSEN, JOHANNES. *Historical Materialism: The Method, the Theories.* New York: Humanities Press, 1960.

676. BABIČ, IVAN. "Blanshard's Reduction of Marxism," *The Journal of Philosophy* 63 (1966), 745–56.
677. BLANSHARD, BRAND. "Reflections on Economic Determinism," *The Journal of Philosophy* 63 (1966), 169–78.
678. BLOOM, SOLOMON F. "Man of His Century: A Reconsideration of the Historical Significance of Karl Marx," *Journal of Political Economy* 51 (1943), 494–505.
679. DANIELOU, JEAN, S. J. "Marxist History and Sacred History," *The Review of Politics* 13 (1951), 503–13.
680. DANIELS, ROBERT V. "Fate and Will in the Marxian Philosophy of History," *Journal of the History of Ideas* 21 (1960), 538–52.
681. DE SELINCOURT, OLIVER. "Some Aspects of the Materialistic Conception of History," *Journal of Philosophical Studies* 2 (1927), 190–204.
682. GARRAGHAN, GILBERT J. "The Materialistic Interpretation of History," *Thought* 14 (1939), 94–112.
683. GRAY, J. L. "Karl Marx and Social Philosophy," in Hearnshaw, F. J. C., ed. *The Social and Political Ideas of Some Representative Thinkers of the Victorian Age.* London: Harrap & Co., 1933. 270p.
684. GUTHRIE, E. F. "Historical Materialism and its Sociological Critics," *Social Forces* 29 (1941), 172–84.

685. HARRIS, ABRAM L. "Economic Evolution: Dialectical and Darwinian," *The Journal of Political Economy* 42 (1934), 34–79.

686. ———. "The Social Philosophy of Karl Marx," *Ethics* 58 (1947–48), 1–42.

687. HARRISON, A. "Marx and Materialism; Reply to Hyndman and Bax," *English Review* 19 (1915), 216–24.

688. HODGEN, MARGARET T. "Karl Marx and the Social Scientists," *Scientific Monthly* 72 (1951), 252–58.

689. KLINE, GEORGE L. "Review of Rodolfo Mondolfo's *Il materialismo storico in Federico Engels,*" *Journal of Philosophy* 51 (1954), 383–89.

690. LEE, HAROLD N. "A Criticism of the Marxian Interpretation of History," *Tulane Studies in Philosophy* 1 (1952), 95–106.

691. MARTIN, KINGSLEY. "Marxism Re-viewed," *The Political Quarterly* 18 (1947), 240–49.

692. MATLEY, IAN M. "The Marxist Approach to the Geographical Environment," *Association of American Geographers, Annals* 56 (1966), 97–111.

693. MAYO, HENRY B. "Marxism as a Philosophy of History," *The Canadian Historical Review* 34 (1953), 1–17.

694. ———. "Marxist Theory and Scientific Methods," *Canadian Journal of Economics* 18 (1952), 487–99.

695. MENDEL, ARTHUR P. "Current Soviet Theory of History: New Trends or Old?" *American Historical Review* 72 (1966), 50–73.

696. ———. "The Rise and Fall of 'Scientific Socialism'," *Foreign Affairs* 45 (1966), 98–111.

697. MIRSKY, D. S. "Bourgeois History and Historical Materialism," *The Labour Monthly* 13 (1931), 451–59.

698. PETTEE, GEORGE S. "The Failure of Marxism," *Journal of Social Philosophy* 6 (1940–41), 101–36.

699. ROSENBERG, HAROLD. "Marxism: Criticism and/or Action" *Dissent* 3 (1956), 366–75.

700. ———. "The Resurrected Romans," *The Kenyon Review* 10 (1948), 602–20.

701. RUSSELL, BERTRAND. "Bolshevik Theory," *The New Republic* 24 (1920), 67–69, 239–41, 296–98.

702. SARAN, A. K. "The Marxian Theory of Social Change," *Inquiry* 6 (1963), 70–128.

703. TUCKER, ROBERT C. "Symbolism of History in Hegel and Marx," *Journal of Philosophy* 54 (1957), 144–45.

704. WILSON, EDMUND. "Marxist History," *The New Republic* 72 (1932), 226–28.

705. BARTOLI, HENRI. *La doctrine économique et sociale de Karl Marx*. Paris: Éditions du Seuil, 1950. 413p.

706. BIGO, PIERRE. *Marxisme et humanisme*. Paris: Presses Universitaires de France, 1953. 269p.

707. BORCHARDT, JULIAN. *Le matérialisme historique*. Bruxelles: L'Églantine, 1931. 71p.

708. GURVITCH, GEORGES. *La vocation actuelle de la sociologie*. Paris: Presses Universitaires de France, 1950. 607p.

709. JAURÈS, JEAN LÉON. *L'idéalisme de l'histoire*. Paris: Imprimerie spéciale, 189–? 35p.

710. LEFÈBVRE, HENRI. *Problèmes actuels du marxisme*. Paris: Presses Universitaires de France, 1958. 126p.

711. MONDOLFO, RODOLFO. *Le matérialisme historique d'après Frederic Engels*. Paris: Études économiques et sociales, 1917. 426p.

712. MONNEROT, JULES. *Sociologie du communisme*. Paris: Gallimard, 1949. 510p.

713. RAPPOPORT, CHARLES. *La philosophie de l'histoire comme science de l'evolution*. Paris: M. Rivière, 1925. 247p.

714. TURGEON, CHARLES H. *Critique de la conception matérialiste de l'histoire*. Paris: Recneil Sirey, 1931. 530p.

715. BETTELHEIM, CHARLES. "Idéologie économique et réalité sociale," *Cahiers Internationaux de Sociologie* 4 (1948), 119–34.

716. DUFRENNE, MIKEL. "Histoire et historicité," *Cahiers Internationaux de Sociologie* 4 (1948), 98–118.

717. ADLER, MAX. *Lehrbuch der materialistischer Geschichtsauffassung*. Berlin: E. Laub, 1930. 2 vols.

718. ———. *Marxistische Probleme*. Stuttgart: Dietz, 1913. 316p.

719. BOGDANOV, ALEKSANDR A. *Die Entwicklungsformen der Gesellschaft und die Wissenschaft*. Berlin: Nike Verlag, 1924. 229p.

720. BRANDENBURG, ERICH A. O. *Die materialistische Geschichtsauffassung, ihr Wesen und ihre Wandlungen*. Leipzig: Quelle & Meyer, 1920. 66p.

721. BRAUNTHAL, ALFRED. *Karl Marx als Geschichtsphilosoph*. Berlin: P. Cassirer, 1920. 194p.

722. BURCK, ERICH, ed. *Die Idee des Fortschritts*. München: C. H. Beck, 1963. 237p.

723. CUNOW, HEINRICH. *Die marxsche Geschichts-, Gesellschafts- und Staatstheorie*. Berlin: Buchhandlung Vorwärts, 1920–21. 2 vols.

724. GORTER, HERMAN. *Der historische Materialismus*. Berlin: Buchhandlung für Arbeiterliteratur, 1928. 137p.

725. GREULICH, HERMANN. *Die materialistische Geschichtsauffassung*. Berlin: Buchhandlung Vorwärts, 1907. 32p.

726. HAMMACHER, EMIL. *Das philosophisch-ökonomische System des Marxismus*. Leipzig: Duncker & Humblot, 1909. 730p.

727. HEIDER, WERNER. *Die Geschichtslehre von Karl Marx*. Stuttgart und Berlin: Cotta, 1931. 201p.

728. HOMMES, JAKOB. *Der technische Eros; das Wesen der materialistischen Geschichtsauffassung*. Freiburg: Herder, 1955. 519p.

729. KAUTSKY, KARL. *Die materialistische Geschichtsauffassung*. Berlin: Dietz, 1927. 2 vols.

730. KHARASOV, GEORG. *Das System des Marxismus*. Berlin: H. Bondy, 1910. 347p.

731. KLEIN, LUDWIG. *Marxismus und Zionismus*. Prag: J. a. verb. "Barissia," 1932. 44p.

732. KRAUSE, GERHARD. *Die Entwicklung der Geschichtsauffassung bis auf Karl Marx*. Berlin: Berliner Arbeiter-Bibliothek, 1891. 46p.

733. KUCZYNSKI, JÜRGEN. *Über einige Probleme des historische Materialismus*. Berlin: Aufbau-Verlag, 1956. 172p.

734. LAFARGUE, PAUL. *Der wirtschaftliche Materialismus nach den Anschauungen von Karl Marx*. Hottingen-Zürich: Volksbuchhandlung, 1896. 37p.

735. LIEBKNECHT, KARL. *Gesammelte Reden und Schriften, 1900–1912*. Berlin: Dietz, 1963. 4 vols.

736. LUKÁCS, GYÖRGY. *Geschichte und Klassenbewusstsien*. Berlin: Malik-Verlag, 1923. 341p.

737. ———. *Schicksalswende; Beiträge zu einer neuen deutschen Ideologie*. Berlin: Aufbau-Verlag, 1956. 253p.

738. MASARYK, THOMAS G. *Die philosophischen und soziologischen Grundlagen des Marxismus*. Wien: C. Konegen, 1899. 600p.

739. MEHNERT, KLAUS. *Weltrevolution durch Weltgeschichte; Die Geschichtslehre des Stalinismus*. Stuttgart: Deutsche Verlag-Anstalt, 1953. 92p.

740. MEHRING, FRANZ. *Gesammelte Schriften*. Berlin: Dietz, 12
    vols. published through 1966.
741. ———. *Über den historischen Materialismus*. Berlin: Dietz,
    1950. 124p.
742. MORF, OTTO. *Das Verhältnis von Wirtschaftstheorie und
    Wirtschaftsgeschichte bei Karl Marx*. Bern: A. Francke,
    1951. 133p.
743. OPPENHEIMER, F. *Das Grundgesetz des Marxschen Gesell-
    schaftslehre*. Berlin: G. Reimer, 1903. 148p.
744. PFOH, WERNER, ed. *Philosophie und Gesellschaft; Beiträge
    zum Studium der marxistischen Philosophie*. Berlin: Aka-
    demie-Verlag, 1958. 518p.
745. STERN, JAKOB. *Der "historische Materialismus" und die "The-
    orie des Mehrwerts" von Karl Marx*. München: M. Ernst,
    1894. 31p.
746. UNTERMANN, ERNEST. *Die logischen Mängel des engeren
    Marxismus*. München: Verlag der Dietzgenschen Philos-
    ophie, 1910. 753p.
747. WEISENGRUEN, PAUL. *Der Marxismus und das Wesen der
    sozialen Frage*. Leipzig: Veit & Co., 1900. 480p.
748. WOLTMANN, LUDWIG. *Der historische Materialismus*. Düssel-
    dorf: Herman Michels, 1900. 430p.

See also: 3, 10, 17, 18, 30, 33, 48, 55, 59, 67, 98, 112, 161, 170, 193,
    194, 202, 221, 228, 320, 324, 327, 329, 336, 374, 387, 414,
    429, 447, 464, 466, 467, 476, 482, 488, 495, 500, 515, 560,
    570, 576, 579, 752, 754, 761, 770, 783, 803, 848, 849, 865,
    917, 920, 926, 931, 934, 954, 971, 990, 991, 992, 996, 999,
    1007, 1011, 1017, 1022, 1023, 1035, 1090, 1135, 1153, 1166,
    1210, 1231, 1239, 1247, 1268, 1304, 1329, 1377, 1414, 1464,
    1480, 1489, 1505, 1509, 1539, 1557.

I2 ———— THE CLASS STRUGGLE

Although the concept of the class struggle plays a central role in historical materialism, few books are dedicated exclusively to its study. For this reason, the number of entries in this section is disproportionate to the importance of its subject matter. There are, however, a substantial number of major discussions of the class war in books whose main subject demanded their classification elsewhere. I have collected these references and listed them under the "See also" rubric at the end of the section.

In 751 a leading Yugoslav Communist, disillusioned, discusses the realities of class structure in Socialist society; the book contains little of theoretical interest. 752 and 754 examine, among others, problems relating to the conflict between the interests of society as a whole and the interests of classes within it. A distinguished Polish social scientist takes an informative look at Marxist and American views of class structure in 753. 756 attempts to account for why Marx saw no role for government by majority rule and free political parties during the transition to communism and in the communist society of the future. 760 gives a reinterpretation of the nature and conditions of class conflict in the terms of contemporary sociology. Parsons argues that although Marx made major contributions to the development of social science, he did not appreciate the stabilizing influence of class structure.

761 is a general examination of the sources of classes and class consciousness; the author of 768 addresses himself to the same topics, but from the Marxist-Leninist point of view. 758 and 759 are searching studies of limited aspects of Marx's theory of class structure. 762 is an informed and informative elucidation of the

Marxist concept of class and the creative, revolutionary activity of the proletariat. 769 contains a brief explication of the fundamental concepts involved in the theory of the class struggle. 766 argues that the elimination of classes and class conflict is neither desirable nor possible. Wright holds the peculiar view that "legitimate" disappointment is an inevitable (and desirable) fact of human existence. 764 makes the claim that the words "class" and "class struggle" are without precise meaning or definition, but the author shows no real acquaintance with Marxist attempts at giving an account of the concept of class. 749 is a major collection of considerable utility. Zetkin's selected works (770) afford important insights into the theory and practice of the class struggle.

749. BENDIX, REINHARD, ed. *Class, Status and Power.* New York: Free Press, 1966. 677p.
750. BOTTOMORE, T. B. *Classes in Modern Society.* New York: Pantheon, 1966. 122p.
751. DJILAS, MILOVAN. *The New Class. An Analysis of the Communist System.* New York: Praeger, 1957. 214p.
752. KAUTSKY, KARL. *The Class Struggle.* Chicago: C. H. Kerr, 1910. 217p.
753. OSSOWSKI, STANISLAW. *Class Structure and Social Consciousness.* New York: The Free Press of Glencoe, 1963. 202p.
754. ROBBINS, LIONEL. *The Economic Basis of Class Conflict.* London: Macmillan, 1939. 277p.
755. SPIRKIN, ALEKSANDR G. *Theoretical Questions of Communist Strategy and Tactics.* Moscow: Novosti Press Agency Publishing House, 1966. 80p.

756. DAHL, ROBERT A. "Marxism and Free Parties," *Journal of Politics* 10 (1948), 787–813.
757. HARRIS, ABRAM L. "Pure Capitalism and the Disappearance of the Middle Class," *The Journal of Political Economy* 47 (1939), 328–56.
758. HODGES, DONALD C. "The 'Intermediate Classes' in Marxian Theory," *Social Research* 28 (1961), 23–36.
759. ———. "The New Class in Marxian Sociology," *Indian Journal of Social Research* 4 (1963), 15–22.
760. PARSONS, TALCOTT. "Social Classes and Class Conflict in the Light of Recent Sociological Theory," *American Economics Review* 39 (1949), 16–26.

761. ROGERS, ARTHUR K. "Class Consciousness," *Ethics* 27 (1917), 334–49.

762. ROSENBERG, HAROLD. "The Pathos of the Proletariat," *The Kenyon Review* 11 (1949), 595–629.

763. SCHUMPETER, JOSEPH A. "The Communist Manifesto in Sociology and Economics," *The Journal of Political Economy* 57 (1949), 199–212.

764. SULZBACH, WALTER. " 'Class' and Class Struggle," *Journal of Social Philosophy* 6 (1940–41), 22–34.

765. WILLIAM, MAURICE. "Is Class Conflict Necessary?" *American Federationist* 29 (1922), 922–25.

766. WRIGHT, DAVID MCCORD. "The Economics of a Classless Society," *American Economics Review* 39 (1949), 27–36.

767. BERTRAND-SERRET, RENÉ. *Le mythe marxiste des "classes."* Paris: Éditions du Cedre, 1955. 234p.

768. CHEREMNYKH, P. *Wie die Klassen enstanden und warum es eine Klassenkampf gibt.* Berlin: Dietz, 1955. 78p.

769. LORENZ, OTTOKAR. *Karl Marx und der Kapitalismus.* Hamburg: Hanseatische Verlagsanstalt, 1937. 135p.

770. ZETKIN, KLARA. *Ausgewählte Reden und Schriften.* Berlin: Dietz, 1957–60. 3 vols.

See also: 4, 6, 17, 36, 48, 67, 170, 174, 191, 202, 209, 221, 320, 327, 367, 426, 467, 488, 495, 538, 639, 640, 642, 647, 656, 661, 663, 668, 673, 698, 699, 701, 711, 714, 722, 729, 734, 735, 736, 828, 834, 848, 857, 866, 891, 893, 903, 906, 1014, 1016, 1069, 1080, 1122, 1268, 1282, 1304, 1401, 1403, 1480, 1539.

I3 — CAPITALISM AND SOCIALISM

The word "socialism" is ambiguous. Sometimes it refers to a group of ideas or theories, at other times to the social movements that aim at actualizing them, at others again to the state of society which would be created if they were fully actualized. The confusion is compounded by the facts that several quite different sets of theories have been called "socialism" and that not all writers are in the habit of explaining clearly which of these theories, social movements, or states of society they have in mind when they attack or defend it. In this section I have attempted to collect a number of works that relate to socialism in two senses of the word. The first is Marxian socialism as a collection of ideas about a desirable future social order and about the steps that should be taken to bring it about. The second is socialism as an actual socio-economic condition of societies which develop according to Marxist-Leninist prescriptions. In this latter sense, socialism is contrasted with capitalism, which it supersedes; it, in turn, will supposedly be superseded by communism.

A clear, Marxist-Leninist explanation of the development of society from capitalism to communism may be found in 774. 788 presents a systematic analysis of the historical materialist view of the political system of capitalism. 804 is a study of Marx's theory of political economy. 795 is a highly readable, charmingly prejudiced introduction. 785 and 826 contain useful material of an introductory nature on the theory of socialism. 777, 790, and 807 are strongly critical of Marxist ideas; the work of Eastman and von Mises appear to be tainted by powerful emotional concerns.

772 is a systematic study of the idea of "utopian" (as distinct

from Marxist) socialism by a leading Jewish theologian. 791 and 830 include assessments of the aims and achievements of German social democracy. For a discussion of the objectives of socialism the reader may turn to 800. 827 is a popular statement of his views by the famous German evolutionary socialist. 794 is an interesting debate; its theoretical contribution, however, is negligible. 796 and 811 are of little philosophical interest.

801 is a group of essays by a Marxist who sees contemporary culture as radically diseased. In his view man in capitalist society understands neither his own nature and wants nor the nature of human liberty. 802 and 803 are analyses of the capitalist socio-economic system that owe a great deal to Marx. In 812 Lord Hailsham offers the opinion that 802 is too close to the views of Marx to be anywhere near the truth about society and history. 806 contains Veblen's essay "The Socialist Economics of Karl Marx and his Followers," along with another valuable article on socialism. 809 compares the views of Mill and Marx concerning the nature and prospects of capitalism. 816 concludes that, in accordance with Marx's prophecy, the contradictions of capitalism will soon bring about its ultimate downfall. By contrast, 810 argues that Marx's theory of the destruction of capitalism has been proved false by the facts.

819 claims that Marxian socialism has made an important contribution to the democratization of modern society. 818 lays special stress on Marx's humanism. 817 is a reprint of a 1911 article in which Luxemburg argues that permanent peace and a United States of Europe are impossible under capitalism. 821 examines the Marxist prediction that under capitalism the condition of the worker will steadily decline. Sowell concludes that this decline need not take the form of a decrease in the amount of goods and services the worker receives. 832 is an account of the progress of East Germany from a capitalist to a socialist form of society. The economic theories underlying Marx's views of the development of society are discussed in 778 as part of an introductory survey; in 824, 829, and 831 they are treated in greater detail. 782 is a philosopher's view of some of Marx's central economic doctrines.

771. ANDERSON, PERRY, ed. *Towards Socialism.* Ithaca, N.Y.: Cornell University Press, 1966. 397p.

772. BUBER, MARTIN. *Paths in Utopia*. London: Routledge and Kegan Paul, 1949. 152p.

773. BURNHAM, JAMES. *The Managerial Revolution: What Is Happening in the World*. New York: John Day, 1941. 285p.

774. BURNS, EMILE. *Capitalism, Communism, and the Transition*. London: V. Gollancz, 1933. 287p.

775. DOBB, MAURICE H. *Political Economy and Capitalism*. London: Routledge, 1937. 359p.

776. DURBIN, EVAN F. M. *The Politics of Democratic Socialism*. London: Routledge, 1940. 384p.

777. EASTMAN, MAX. *Reflections on the Failure of Socialism*. New York: Devin-Adair, 1955. 127p.

778. GRAY, SIR ALEXANDER. *The Development of Economic Doctrine*. New York: Wiley, 1961. 384p.

779. GROSS, FELIKS, ed. *European Ideologies: A Survey of 20th Century Political Ideas*. New York: Philosophical Library, 1948. 1075p.

780. HALÉVY, ÉLIE. *The Era of Tyrannies*. Garden City, N.Y.: Anchor, 1965. 324p.

781. HUBERMAN, LEO. *The Truth about Socialism*. New York: Lear Publishers, 1950. 256p.

782. JOSEPH, HORACE W. B. *The Labour Theory of Value in Karl Marx*. London: Oxford, 1923. 176p.

783. LABRIOLA, ANTONIO. *Socialism and Philosophy*. Chicago: Kerr, 1907. 260p.

784. LAFARGUE, PAUL. *Social and Philosophical Studies*. Chicago: Kerr, 1906. 165p.

785. LASKI, HAROLD J. *An Introduction to Politics*. London: Allen and Unwin, 1931. 112p.

786. LICHTMAN, RICHARD. *Toward Community: A Criticism of Contemporary Capitalism*. Santa Barbara, Calif.: Center for the Study of Democratic Institutions, 1966. 58p.

787. MACDONALD, JAMES R. *Socialism and Society*. London: Independent Labor Party, 1906. 186p.

788. MOORE, STANLEY W. *The Critique of Capitalist Democracy*. New York: Paine-Whitman, 1957. 180p.

789. PLEKHANOV, GEORGII V. *Anarchism and Socialism*. Chicago: Kerr, 1909. 148p.

790. REID, DAVID C. *Capital and Profits*. Springfield, Mass.: The Hazard Co., 1914. 221p.

791. RUSSELL, BERTRAND. *German Social Democracy*. New York: Longmans, Green, 1896. 204p.

792. SALTER, FRANK R. *Karl Marx and Modern Socialism.* London: Macmillan, 1921. 263p.

793. SCOTT, JOHN W. *Karl Marx on Value.* London: A. & C. Black, 1920. 54p.

794. SELIGMAN, EDWIN R. A. *Debate: "Is the Failure of Socialism ... Due to the Fallacies of Marxian Theory?".* Affirmative: Edwin R. A. Seligman. Negative: Harry Waton. New York: Marx-Engels Institute, 1922. 62p.

795. SHAW, GEORGE B. *The Intelligent Woman's Guide to Socialism and Capitalism.* New York: Brentano's, 1928. 495p.

796. SIMKHOVITCH, VLADIMIR G. *Marxism versus Socialism.* New York: Henry Holt, 1913. 298p.

797. SOCIALIST LABOUR PARTY OF GREAT BRITAIN. NATIONAL EXEC-UTIVE COUNCIL. *Marxism versus Stalinism.* Edinburgh: Socialist Labour Press, 1950. 34p.

798. SOMBART, WERNER. *Socialism and Social Movement.* New York: Dutton, 1909. 319p.

799. SPARGO, JOHN. *Sidelights on Contemporary Socialism.* New York: B. W. Huebsch, 1911. 154p.

800. ———. *Substance of Socialism.* New York: B. W. Huebsch, 1909. 162p.

801. SPRIGG, CHRISTOPHER S. (CAUDWELL, CHRISTOPHER, pseud.). *Studies in a Dying Culture.* London: John Lane, 1948. 228p.

802. STRACHEY, JOHN. *Contemporary Capitalism.* New York: Random House, 1956. 374p.

803. ———. *The Nature of Capitalist Crisis.* New York: Covici, Friede, 1935. 400p.

804. SWEEZY, PAUL M. *The Theory of Capitalist Development.* New York: Oxford University Press, 1942. 398p.

805. TORR, DONA, ed. *Marxism, Nationality and War.* London: Lawrence & Wishart, 1941. 2 vols.

806. VEBLEN, THORSTEIN. *The Place of Science in Modern Civilization and Other Essays.* New York: B. W. Huebsch, 1919. 509p.

807. VON MISES, LUDWIG. *Socialism; An Economic and Sociological Analysis.* New Haven: Yale University Press, 1951. 599p.

808. WOLFSON, MURRAY. *A Reappraisal of Marxian Economics.* New York: Columbia University Press, 1966. 220p.

809. BLADEN, V. W. "Centenary of Marx and Mill," *Journal of Economic History* 8 (1948), 32–41.

810. COMMONS, JOHN R. "Marx Today: Capitalism and Socialism," *Atlantic Monthly* 136 (1925), 682–93.

811. FELLNER, ERNST. "The Psychology of Socialism," *Hibbert Journal* 46 (1947), 138–45.

812. HAILSHAM, LORD. "Half-Lapsed Heretic," *The Spectator* 6681 (1956), 56–57.

813. HOOK, SIDNEY. "Socialism and Liberation," *The Partisan Review* 24 (1957), 497–518.

814. HYNDMAN, H. M. "The Coming Triumph of Marxist Socialism," *English Review* 19 (1915), 290–304.

815. HYNDMAN, H. M. and BAX, E. B. "Socialism, Materialism and War," *English Review* 19 (1914), 52–61.

816. LEWIS, ALFRED B. "The Mills of Marx Grind Slowly," *The Christian Century* 53 (1936), 669–701.

817. LUXEMBURG, ROSA. "Peace Utopias," *The Labour Monthly* 8 (1926), 421–28.

818. PARSONS, HOWARD L. "Value and Mental Health in the Thought of Marx," *Philosophy and Phenomenological Research* 24 (1964), 355–65.

819. SMALL, ALBION W. "Socialism in the Light of Social Science," *The American Journal of Sociology* 17 (1911–12), 804–19.

820. SMITH, T. V. "Social Intelligence and the Communistic Experiment," *Ethics* 42 (1931–32), 113–31.

821. SOWELL, THOMAS. "Marx's Increasing Misery Doctrine," *American Economic Review* 50 (1960), 111–20.

822. WEAKLAND, JOHN H. "Family Imagery in a Passage by Mao Tse-tung: an Essay in Psycho-cultural Method," *World Politics* 10 (1958), 387–407.

823. COGNIOT, GEORGES. *Actualité du "Capital": la nécessité sociale et l'action humaine.* Paris: Éditions sociales, 1948. 46p.

824. GUIHÉNEUF, ROBERT. *Le problème de la théorie marxiste de la valeur.* Paris: A. Colin, 1952. 194p.

825. LEFÈBVRE, HENRI. "Marxisme et sociologie," *Cahiers Internationaux de Sociologie* 4 (1948), 48–74.

826. BAUER, OTTO. *Kapitalismus und Sozialismus nach dem Weltkrieg.* Wien: Wiener Volksbuchhandlung, 1931.

827. BERNSTEIN, EDUARD. *Wie ist wissenschaftlicher Sozialismus möglich?* Berlin: Verlag der Sozialistischen Monatshefte, 1901. 50p.

828. HELLWEG, MARTIN. *Die Stellung des Proletariats bei Karl Marx*. Frankfurt am Main: G. Schulte-Bulunke, 1947. 31p.
829. KÖPPEL, LEO. *Grenznutzentheorie und Marxismus*. Leipzig und Wien: F. Deuticke, 1930. 98p.
830. LORENZ, MAX. *Die marxistische Sozialdemokratie*. Leipzig: G. H. Wigand, 1896. 229p.
831. PETRY, FRANZ. *Der soziale Gehalt der Marxschen Werttheorie*. Jena: G. Fischer, 1916. 70p.
832. ULBRICHT, WALTER. *Über die Dialektik unseres sozialistischen Aufbaus*. Berlin: Dietz, 1959. 316p.

See also: 2, 6, 17, 34, 36, 46, 54, 63, 174, 190, 202, 215, 279, 320, 335, 340, 350, 399, 645, 647, 651, 717, 723, 753, 755, 757, 769, 844, 854, 860, 880, 910, 994, 1018, 1031, 1047, 1137, 1148, 1387, 1389, 1401, 1403, 1447, 1467, 1480, 1511.

14 —— MARXISM, DEMOCRACY, AND THE DICTATORSHIP OF THE PROLETARIAT

A good discussion of Marxist political philosophy may be found in 848; 854 makes some valuable contributions to the comparative study of social structures. Both books, however, fall short of being authoritative in their fields. 845 should be read by everyone who is seriously interested in the idea of the dictatorship of the proletariat. 857 is an important document on Marxist–Leninist theory and practice.

833 is an undistinguished monograph of the recently established American Institute for Marxist Studies. As usual, Arendt's writing

(834) leaves one with the feeling that she is *almost* right—but not quite. 835 contains more psychological than philosophical material. 837, 839, 840, and 858 are weak; 838 is also unconvincing. 841 is a book of some substance, and its analysis of totalitarianism is of considerable interest. 846 attempts to show that Marxism and the democratic tradition are not as far apart as it has sometimes been supposed. Murry (852) defends something he calls "democracy" against all comers.

849 is a series of essays on democracy which resulted from a UNESCO questionnaire sent to over five hundred experts. Of special interest are Bober's discussion of the Marxian notion of democracy, Lefèbvre's account of Marxist-Leninist political philosophy, and Plamenatz's examination of Marxian "proletarian democracy." 856 is a philosophically inadequate comparison of Western liberal theory and practice with Marx's thought and its embodiment in the Communist world. 859 is a draft program for the Third Communist International, describing the road to be followed through revolution to the dictatorship of the proletariat. 860 analyses the relationship of democracy to the capitalist and to the socialist economic system.

833. APTHEKER, HERBERT, ed. *Marxism and Democracy: A Symposium.* New York: Humanities Press, 1965. 114p.

834. ARENDT, HANNAH. *The Origins of Totalitarianism.* New York: Meridian Books, 1958. 520p.

835. BARBU, ZEVEDEI. *Democracy and Dictatorship.* New York: Grove Press, 1956. 275p.

836. BLANSHARD, PAUL. *Communism, Democracy and Catholic Power.* Boston: Beacon Press, 1951. 340p.

837. BOHLMAN, MARY EDNA. *Democracy and Its Competitors.* Columbus, Ohio: Charles E. Merrill, 1962. 80p.

838. COLEGROVE, KENNETH W. *Democracy Versus Communism.* Princeton, N. J.: Van Nostrand, 1961. 442p.

839. EBENSTEIN, WILLIAM. *Two Ways of Life: The Communist Challenge to Democracy.* New York: Holt, Rinehart and Winston, 1962. 406p.

840. FEAREY, ROBERT A. *The U.S. Versus the U.S.S.R.: Ideologies in Conflict.* Washington, D.C.: Public Affairs Press, 1959. 48p.

841. FRIEDRICH, CARL J., and BRZEZINSKI, Z. K. *Totalitarian Dictatorship and Autocracy*. New York: Praeger, 1961. 346p.
842. HAVENS, MURRAY C. *The Challenges to Democracy*. Austin: University of Texas Press, 1965. 119p.
843. HEIMANN, ÉDUARD. *Communism, Fascism, or Democracy?* New York: Norton, 1938. 288p.
844. HIRSCH, MAX. *Democracy vs. Socialism*. New York: Macmillan, 1901. 481p.
845. KAUTSKY, KARL. *The Dictatorship of the Proletariat*. Ann Arbor, Mich.: University of Michigan Press, 1964. 192p.
846. LANDY, A. *Marxism and the Democratic Tradition*. New York: International Publishers, 1946. 220p.
847. LAURAT, LUCIEN. *Marxism and Democracy*. London: V. Gollancz, 1940. 254p.
848. MAYO, HENRY B. *Democracy and Marxism*. New York: Oxford University Press, 1955. 364p.
849. McKEON, RICHARD, ed. *Democracy in a World of Tensions*. Chicago: University of Chicago Press, 1951. 540p.
850. MOORE, BARRINGTON. *Social Origins of Dictatorship and Democracy*. Boston: Beacon Press, 1966. 559p.
851. [not used]
852. MURRY, JOHN M. *The Defense of Democracy*. London: J. Cape, 1939. 315p.
853. RUBINSTEIN, ALVIN Z. *Communist Political Systems*. Englewood Cliffs, N.J.: Prentice-Hall, 1966. 399p.
854. SCHUMPETER, JOSEPH A. *Capitalism, Socialism and Democracy*. New York: Harper, 1947. 431p.
855. SPARGO, JOHN. *Bolshevism, the Enemy of Political and Industrial Democracy*. New York: Harper, 1919. 389p.
856. TAYLOR, OVERTON H. *The Classical Liberalism, Marxism and the Twentieth Century*. Cambridge, Mass.: Harvard University Press, 1960. 122p.
857. TROTSKII, LEV D. *Terrorism and Communism*. Ann Arbor, Mich.: University of Michigan Press, 1961. 420p.
858. U.S. CONGRESS. HOUSE COMMITTEE ON UN-AMERICAN ACTIVITIES. *The Ideology of Freedom vs. the Ideology of Communism*. Washington, D.C.: U.S. Government Printing Office, 1958. 22p.

859. BUKHARIN, NIKOLAI I. "A Programme of Marxism," *The Labour Monthly* 4 (1923), 75–92.
860. KELSEN, HANS. "Foundations of Democracy. III. Democracy and Economics," *Ethics* 66 (1955–56), 68–94.

861. LOWENTHAL, RICHARD. "Totalitarianism Reconsidered," *Commentary* 29 (1960), 504–12.

862. MANUILSKII, DMITRII Z. *Der Marxismus als Lehre von der proletarischen Diktatur.* Moskau-Leningrad: Verlagsgenossenschaft ausländischer Arbeiter in der UdSSR, 1933. 32p.

See also: 17, 48, 63, 151, 426, 642, 661, 701, 717, 723, 755, 756, 780, 788, 914, 937, 993, 1009, 1025, 1147, 1521.

15 ———————————— THE STATE

The classic Marxist-Leninist work on the nature, function, and future of the state is Lenin's *The State and Revolution* (48). For contrast the reader might consult the anarchist Bakunin's 863; for direct criticism Bakunin's 864. 865 is a careful study of Marx's ideas about the historical role of nations and nationalism.

866, 870, 871, 881, 883, and 884 are largely expository in character: they offer very little new. Although the title of 866 suggests that its topic is Marx's theory of the state, the view actually discussed is the Marxist-Leninist one. The book contains a chapter on the application of this theory in the Soviet Union. 867 draws instructive contrasts between the Soviet and the Yugoslav views of the nature and function of the state. 872 is an excellent analysis of the shifts that occurred under Stalin in the Soviet conception of the state and of the role of social consciousness in social change. The author argues that Marxist-Leninist theories in these fields have been either abandoned or inverted until they resemble Hegel more closely than they resemble Marx.

The point of 874 is that there is no withering away of the state in the Soviet Union today. The alleged discrepancy between the Marxist-Leninist theory of the withering away of the state and actual Soviet practice is "one of the most fantastic contradictions in the history of human institutions," according to 875. 876 raises some important general questions but fails, along with the rest of the literature, to subject the Marxist-Leninist theory of the state to the sort of critical scrutiny that could identify and defend its strengths, expose its weaknesses, and render a reasoned judgment on its adequacy as a whole. 877 is an important contribution; Barion's work (878) is particularly useful for the person interested in a comparison and contrast of the Hegelian and Marxist views of the state.

863. BAKUNIN, MIKHAIL. *God and the State*. New York: Mother Earth Publishing Association, 1916 (?). 86p.

864. ———. *Marxism, Freedom and the State*. London: Freedom Press, 1950. 63p.

865. BLOOM, SOLOMON F. *The World of Nations: A Study in the National Implications in the Work of Karl Marx*. New York: Columbia University Press, 1941. 225p.

866. CHANG, SHERMAN H. *The Marxian Theory of the State*. Philadelphia: Privately printed, 1931. 230p.

867. LAPENNA, IVO. *State and Law: Soviet and Yugoslav Theory*. New Haven: Yale University Press, 1964. 135p.

868. [not used]

869. THOMPSON, RONALD B. *Lenin's Theory of the State, 1914–1916*. Chicago: Department of Photographic Reproduction, University of Chicago, 1954 (?). 166 l.

870. VYSHINSKII, ANDREI I. *J. V. Stalin's Doctrine of the Socialist State*. Moscow: Foreign Languages Publishing House, 1951. 63p.

871. ———. *The Teachings of Lenin and Stalin on the Proletarian Revolution and the State*. London: Soviet News, 1948. 120p.

872. ASPATURIAN, VERNON V. "Contemporary Doctrine of the Soviet State and its Philosophical Foundations," *American Political Science Review* 48 (1954), 1031–57.

873. BLOOM, SOLOMON F. "The 'Withering Away' of the State," *The Journal of the History of Ideas* 7 (1946), 113–21.

874. BRINKLEY, GEORGE A. "The 'Withering' of the State under

Khrushchev," *The Review of Politics* 23 (1961), 37–51.
875. HOOVER, CALVIN B. "The Soviet State Fails to Wither," *Foreign Affairs* 31 (1952), 114–27.
876. STRACHEY, JOHN. "Liberty and the Modern State," *Aristotelian Society Supplementary Volume* 13 (1934), 31–41.

877. ADLER, MAX. *Die Staatsauffassung des Marxismus*. Darmstadt: Wissenschaftliche Buchgesellschaft, 1964. 315p.
878. BARION, JAKOB. *Hegel und die marxistische Staatslehre*. Bonn: Bouview, 1963. 235p.
879. DAHRENDORF, RALF. *Marx in Perspektiv*. Hannover: Dietz, 1953. 186p.
880. GUMPLOWICZ, LUDWIG. *Rechtsstaat und Sozialismus*. Innsbruck: Wagner, 1881. 548p.
881. HIPPLER, FRITZ. *Staat und Gesellschaft bei Mill, Marx, Lagarde*. Berlin: Jünker und Dunnhaupt, 1934. 239p.
882. KELSEN, HANS. *Sozialismus und Staat*. Leipzig: Hirschfeld, 1923. 208p.
883. TURETSKII, V. A. *Die Entwicklung der Anschauungen von Marx und Engels über den Staat*. Berlin: Deutscher Zentralverlag, 1956. 116p.
884. VORLÄNDER, KARL. *Von Machiavelli bis Lenin: neuzeitliche Staats-und Gesellschaftstheorien*. Leipzig: Quelle & Meyer, 1926. 286p.

See also: 33, 47, 48, 52, 174, 324, 327, 653, 660, 717, 723, 788, 834, 841, 853, 861, 889, 937, 1029, 1048, 1114, 1118.

16 ———————— REVOLUTION

One of the central issues emerging from the application of Marxist materialism to the study of history is that of the role of revolutions in promoting social progress. Marxist-Leninists believe that no progress and no genuine improvement of the lot of the workingman is possible without the destruction of existing productive relations and of the repressive mechanisms of the state. One of the major forms of revisionism, on the other hand, maintains that reforms attainable under existing social and political conditions suffice to relieve the plight of the proletariat and that revolution is, therefore, both unnecessary and undesirable. This problem is discussed in some detail in 886, 890, and 893. 887 and 896 are accounts of the Russian revolution from the standpoint of the social theories of which it was the direct practical issue.

Although Marx thought that the proletarian revolution would be brought about by a spontaneous uprising of the oppressed, Lenin realized the central role that would have to be played by organized cadres of Communist intellectuals. This and related issues are discussed in 892, 899, 901, and to some extent in Wolfe's exciting narrative (900). 905 makes an able attempt to show how Marxist doctrine may be interpreted to require the action of a revolutionary intelligentsia. 909 discusses the relation of philosophy to revolution. 906 is an account of the difference between Marx's and Lenin's conceptions of the role of war in the development of society. 898 is a study of nineteenth- and twentieth-century revolutionaries from Blanqui to Stalin. 888 contains Camus' important distinction between revolt and revolution.

885. APTHEKER, HERBERT. *The Nature of Revolution.* New York: New Century Publishers, 1959. 31p.
886. ARENDT, HANNAH. *On Revolution.* London: Faber & Faber, 1963. 343p.
887. BERDIAEV, NIKOLAI A. *The Russian Revolution.* Ann Arbor, Mich.: University of Michigan Press, 1960. 96p.
888. CAMUS, ALBERT. *The Rebel.* New York: Knopf, 1954. 273p.
889. CARR, EDWARD H. *Studies in Revolution.* New York: Grosset & Dunlap, 1964. 227p.
890. DELEON, DANIEL. *Reform or Revolution.* New York: Socialist Labor Party, 1924. 32p.
891. DRACHKOVITCH, MILORAD M., ed. *The Revolutionary Internationals, 1864–1943.* Stanford: Stanford University Press for Hoover Institution on War, Revolution, and Peace, 1966. 256p.

892. EASTMAN, MAX. *Marx, Lenin and the Science of Revolution.* London: Allen and Unwin, 1926. 267p.

893. KAUTSKY, KARL. *The Social Revolution.* Chicago: C. H. Kerr, 1908. 189p.

894. LAMPERT, EVGENII. *Studies in Rebellion.* New York: Praeger, 1957. 295p.

895. LASKI, HAROLD J. *Reflections on the Revolution of our Time.* New York: Viking, 1943. 419p.

896. LUXEMBURG, ROSA. *The Russian Revolution.* New York: Workers Age, 1940. 56p.

897. MAGUIRE, JAMES J. *The Philosophy of Modern Revolution.* Washington, D.C.: Catholic University of America Press, 1943. 188p.

898. NOMAD, MAX. *Apostles of Revolution.* Boston: Little, Brown, 1939. 467p.

899. TROTSKII, LEV D. *The Permanent Revolution.* New York:

900. WOLFE, BERTRAM D. *Three Who Made A Revolution.* New Pioneer Publishers, 1931. 157p.
York: Dial Press, 1960. 661p.

901. BECKER, FRANCES B. "Lenin's Application of Marx's Theory on Revolutionary Tactics," *American Sociological Review* 2 (1937), 353–64.

902. BURNS, C. D. "Karl Marx and Revolution," *English Review* 31 (1920), 244–53.

903. ELLIOTT, CHARLES F. "Lenin, Rosa Luxembourg and the Dilemma of the Non-Revolutionary Proletariat," *Midwest Journal of Political Science* 9 (1965), 327–38.

904. GAUTHIER, D. D. "The Philosophy of Revolution," *University of Toronto Quarterly* 22 (1963), 126–41.

905. HEIMANN, EDWARD. "Marxism and Underdeveloped Countries," *Social Research* 19 (1952), 322–45.

906. WOLFE, BERTRAM D. " 'War is the Womb of Revolution': Lenin 'Consults' Hegel," *Antioch Review* 16 (1956), 190–97.

907. IZARD, GEORGES. *L'homme est révolutionnaire.* Paris: B. Grasset, 1945. 315p.

908. AHLBERG, RENÉ. *Weltrevolution durch Koexistenz.* Berlin: Colloquium Verlag, 1962. 78p.

909. Luppol, Ivan K. *Lenin und die Philosophie.* Berlin: Universum-Bücherei für Alle, 1931. 256p.

See also: 17, 34, 43, 48, 75, 111, 170, 174, 221, 324, 327, 343, 495, 568, 641, 653, 658, 660, 701, 713, 717, 723, 729, 735, 736, 739, 762, 774, 845, 848, 849, 857, 866, 871, 972, 984, 1077, 1106, 1298, 1305, 1306, 1308, 1328, 1387, 1389, 1391, 1395, 1399, 1403, 1445.

17 ——————— SUBSTRUCTURE, SUPERSTRUCTURE, AND IDEOLOGY

The best discussion of the Marxist-Leninist view of the relation of the economic substructure to the ideological superstructure may be found in 917. Acton's incisive analysis goes a long way toward clarifying the confused claims sometimes made about the economic conditioning of the artistic and intellectual life of societies. Much weaker discussions may be found in 913 and 926. 915 and 922 examine the relationship of socio-economic reality to art. 920 argues that not even the development of social life may be explained by Marx's theory: even there biological and psychological factors play a more significant causal role than economic ones.

If philosophy is a part of the ideological superstructure and no ideology can provide objective truths, the philosophy of Marxism-Leninism must bring its own truth into question. This problem is discussed in 912 and in a chapter on the concept of ideology in the thought of Marx in 924. 921 raises the same problem about Marxist-Leninist social science: its dual character derives from its claims to provide both absolute and objective, and relative and partisan truths. 919 maintains that Marxist-Leninist ideology is solely an instrument of power for the Communist Party; 911 is a more serious study of the relationship of ideology and power in the Soviet Union. 918 maintains that Marxism is a romantic view tainted with the subjectivity of social class consciousness. 923 is a serious exploration of the idea of ideology; 910 is an examination of its social role and future.

910. BELL, DANIEL. *The End of Ideology.* Glencoe, Ill.: Free Press, 1960. 416p.
911. BRZEZINSKI, ZBIGNIEW K. *Ideology and Power in Soviet Politics.* New York: Praeger, 1962. 180p.
912. HOROWITZ, IRVING L. *Philosophy, Science, and the Sociology of Knowledge.* Springfield, Ill.: C. C. Thomas, 1961. 169p.
913. KONSTANTINOV, F. V. *Basis and Superstructure.* Moscow: Foreign Languages Publishing House, n.d.
914. PETERSEN, WILLIAM, ed. *The Realities of World Communism.* Englewood Cliffs, N.J.: Prentice-Hall, 1963. 222p.
915. PLEKHANOV, GEORGII V. *Art and Social Life.* London: Lawrence & Wishart, 1953. 235p.
916. SKARD, YVIND. *Ideological Strategy.* London: Blandford Press, 1954 (?). 79p.

917. ACTON, H. B. "The Materialist Conception of History," *Proceedings of the Aristotelian Society* 52 (1951–52), 207–24.
918. BARBU, ZEVEDEI. "Marxist Philosophy and European Thought," *Philosophical Quarterly* 3 (1953), 150–66.
919. COSER, LEWIS, and HOWE, IRVING. "The Role of Ideology," *Dissent* 4 (1957), 376–81.
920. ELLWOOD, CHARLES A. "Marx's 'Economic Determinism' in the Light of Modern Psychology," *American Journal of Sociology* 17 (1911), 35–46.
921. HODGES, DONALD C. "The Dual Character of Marxian Social Science," *Philosophy of Science* 29 (1962), 333–49.
922. KAVOLIS, V. "Art Content and Economic Reality," *The American Journal of Economics and Sociology* 24 (1965), 321–28.
923. LICHTHEIM, GEORGE. "The Concept of Ideology," *History and Theory* 4 (1965), 164–95.

924. BARTH, HANS. *Wahrheit und Ideologie.* Zürich: Manesse Verlag, 1945. 350p.

925. HÜRLIMANN, OTTO. *Ideologie und Methode des Kommunismus.* Zürich: Kommissionsverlag Gotthelf-Verlag, 1951. 29p.

926. JAKUBOWSKI, FRANZ. *Der ideologische Überbau in der materialistischen Geschichtsauffassung.* Danzig: Anton Fooken, 1936. 122p.

See also: 48, 245, 357, 397, 523, 524, 656, 669, 714, 717, 723, 736, 848, 858, 872, 962, 1055, 1068, 1069, 1073, 1074, 1078, 1082, 1090, 1093, 1135, 1152, 1168, 1184, 1247, 1248, 1280, 1365, 1480.

18 —— THE UNITY OF THEORY AND PRACTICE

The phrase "unity of theory and practice" has two distinct meanings. (1) It is sometimes taken to refer to the Marxist-Leninist view that the activity of theorizing and practical human action are inextricably interwoven. (2) At other times it is used to refer to the relationship between the body of Marxist-Leninist theories and their actual application in the Soviet Union. (1) is a substitution instance, albeit a very important one, of the general dialectical materialist principle of the unity of opposites. Unfortunately, there are very few discussions of it in the literature. (2), on the other hand, is amply examined; studies of it, however, offer only limited philosophical enlightenment.

940 is an important, monograph-length examination of the concepts of theory and practice in the philosophical development of Marx from his student days to *The German Ideology*. Other significant discussions of the philosophical theory of unified theory and practice may be found in 934 and 938. 932 and 933 present an

elaboration of how theory may be translated into action. 928 demonstrates how the aims and practical policies of the Russian Communist Party derive from Marxist-Leninist philosophy.

930 is a useful introductory presentation of the philosophical views of Engels and Marx. The author traces the practical application of Marx's social and political theories from their formulation to the Stalinist years. 931 views the development of Marxian social theory (and its application) from its antecedents at the time of the French Revolution to its alleged dissolution in contemporary Russia. 927, 929, 935, and 937 take firmly critical views of the discrepancy between Marxist-Leninist theory and actual Soviet practice. 936 contains a wealth of valuable information, but little that is philosophically new.

927. BOUSCAREN, ANTHONY T. *Communism: Theory and Practice*. New York: Paulist Press, 1960. 32p.

928. BUKHARIN, NIKOLAI I., and PREOBRAZHENSKY, EVGENII. *The ABC of Communism*. London: The Communist Party of Great Britain, 1922. 422p.

929. GURIAN, WALDEMAR. *Bolshevism: Theory and Practice*. New York: Macmillan, 1932. 402p.

930. HUNT, ROBERT N. C. *The Theory and Practice of Communism, an Introduction*. New York: Macmillan, 1961. 231p.

931. LICHTHEIM, GEORGE. *Marxism: An Historical and Critical Study*. New York: Praeger, 1961. 412p.

932. MAO, TSE-TUNG. *On Practice*. Peking: Foreign Language Press, 1958. 21p.

933. ———. *On the Correct Handling of Contradictions Among the People*. Peking: Foreign Language Press, 1960. 69p.

934. MEYER, ALFRED G. *Marxism: The Unity of Theory and Practice*. Cambridge, Mass.: Harvard University Press, 1954. 181p.

935. RUSSELL, BERTRAND. *The Practice and Theory of Bolshevism*. London: Allen & Unwin, 1921. 188p.

936. SHAFFER, H. G., ed. *The Soviet System in Theory and Practice*. New York: Appleton-Century-Crofts, 1965. 470p.

937. COLE, GEORGE D. H. "What Has Happened to Marxism?" *The New Republic* 126 (1952): I (March 17), 13–15; II (March 24), 9–11.

938. McGILL, V. J. "Notes on Theory and Practice in Marxist Philosophy," *Philosophy and Phenomenological Research* 5 (1944–45), 217–41.

939. LÖWENTHAL, FRITZ. *Das kommunistische Experiment: Theorie und Praxis des Marxismus-Leninismus.* Köln: Markus Verlag, 1957. 280p.

940. RÖTTCHER, FEODOR. "Theorie und Praxis in den Frühschriften von Karl Marx," *Archiv für Philosophie* 11 (1962), 246–311.

See also: 465, 495, 576, 717, 723, 736, 853, 955, 962, 1298, 1393, 1416, 1480, 1506.

19 ——— THE NATURE OF MAN

For a system of thought that lays claim to completeness and intends to provide an account of the good life, no issue can be more central than that of the nature of man. It is surprising, therefore, that to this date only fragmentary examinations, defenses, and critiques of the Marxist-Leninist view have appeared in print. Among the expositions 966 provides a useful bird's-eye view. 944 is an excellent group of selections from the 1844 Manuscripts; but Fromm's introduction lacks philosophical rigor. 948 undertakes the important task of extracting a theory of the nature of man from the writings of Engels and Marx; but the book contains too many direct quotes and neither sustained analysis nor evaluation. Schaff's recent work (945) is tantalizing in its promise; unfortunately, it leaves many more problems untouched than it manages to resolve. 955 is an interesting essay by a leading Yugoslav philosopher, but it suffers from the vagueness of some of its central concepts. Garaudy's work (961) is too general to be of much value as an analysis; his comparisons, however, are instructive.

941 and 952 are careful and informed studies of Soviet assumptions about the nature of man. The former contains some shrewd observations about the assumptions of Soviet leaders; the latter is of more immediate philosophical interest. 959 is a highly informative discussion of the Stalinist attempt to establish a scientific basis for the transformation and control of human nature. Tucker is successful in showing the relevance of Pavlovian psychology, Lysenko's theory of biology, and Stalin's view of linguistics to a unifying concept of man.

There has been a considerable amount of criticism of the Marxist view from the standpoint of Thomistic philosophy. 963 contrasts Marx's view of the nature of man with that of St. Thomas Aquinas. The contrast would be instructive if its outcome were not obvious from the first. 946 and 947 are other Roman Catholic critiques of limited philosophical value. Tillich's treatment (967) of the similarities and differences between the Marxist and the Christian views of man is only a beginning. 950 argues that Marxist humanism fails because it leaves out of account the spiritual element in man's nature. 962 and 964 are critical of the Marxist-Leninist view, but both lack the sustained analytic scrutiny necessary for backing up any claim of its inadequacy. 954 is a withering attack on the Soviet philosopher Mitin's paper read to the Twelfth International Philosophical Congress. Hook argues that Mitin's views about nature, man, society, history, and science are fraught with ambiguity and error.

949 maintains the remarkable view that Teilhard de Chardin, Marx, and Eastern religions basically all agree about the nature of man. 951 is a loose account of the dialectical materialist theory of human nature. Harris (953) presents a weak analysis of Marx's concept of freedom, and the relation of labor to man's nature and development. He concludes that worker control of industry and abolition of the division of labor are impracticable goals. 957 attempts to exhibit Marx's view of man as the ultimate result of liberalism in metaphysics and ethics. What such liberalism might be is not explained. 958 is an able critique of Arendt's statements concerning the Marxian view of man and labor.

A brief review of the available literature should be adequate to show to the serious reader the dearth of substantial work in this central field and to convince him of the need for an extended, philosophically unbiased examination of the Marxist theory of the nature of man.

941. CANTRIL, HADLEY. *Soviet Leaders and Mastery Over Man.* New Brunswick, N.J.: Rutgers University Press, 1960. 173p.

942. DAVENPORT, RUSSELL W. *The Dignity of Man.* New York: Harper, 1955. 338p.

943. DOHERTY, JOHN J. *The Concept of Man in Communist Philosophy.* Washington, D.C.: The Catholic University of America Press, 1955. 33p.

944. FROMM, ERICH, ed. *Marx's Concept of Man.* New York: Ungar, 1961. 260p.

945. SCHAFF, ADAM. *A Philosophy of Man.* New York: Monthly Review Press, 1963. 139p.

946. SCHEUER, MARCELLUS J. *Philosophy of Man in Communism.* Washington, D.C.: Catholic University of America Press, 1952. Microcard.

947. SHEED, FRANCIS J. *Communism and Man.* New York: Sheed and Ward, 1938. 247p.

948. VENABLE, VERNON. *Human Nature: the Marxian View.* New York: Knopf, 1945. 213p.

949. ZAEHNER, R. C. *Matter and Spirit.* New York: Harper & Row, 1963. 210p.

950. BERDIAEV, NIKOLAI A. "Spiritual Dualism and Daily Bread," *The American Scholar* 7 (1938), 223–29.

951. DAVENPORT, RUSSELL W. "The Real Power Behind Communism," *Fortune* 51 (1955), 133–35, 150–60.

952. DE GEORGE, RICHARD T. "The Soviet Concept of Man," *Iris Hibernia* (1964), 14–28.

953. HARRIS, ABRAM L. "Utopian Elements in Marx's Thought," *Ethics* 60 (1950), 79–99.

954. HOOK, SIDNEY. "Man and Nature: Some Questions for Mr. Mitin," *Journal of Philosophy* 56 (1959), 408–15.

955. PETROVIĆ, GAJO. "Man as Economic Animal and Man as Praxis," *Inquiry* 6 (1963), 35–56.

956. REID, J. P. "Marx on the Unity of Man," *The Thomist* 28 (1964), 259–301.

957. ROTHMAN, STANLEY. "Marxism and the Paradox of Contemporary Political Thought," *The Review of Politics* 24 (1962), 212–32.
958. SUCHTING, W. A. "Marx and Hannah Arendt's *The Human Condition*," *Ethics* 73 (1962), 47–55.
959. TUCKER, ROBERT C. "Stalin and the Uses of Psychology," *World Politics* 8 (1956), 455–83.

960. GARAUDY, ROGER. *Le marxisme et la personne humaine*. Paris: Éditions sociales, 1949. 33p.
961. ——. *Perspectives de l'homme: existentialisme, pensée catholique, marxisme*. Paris: Presses Universitaires de France, 1960. 359p.

962. BOCHEŃSKI, INNOCENTIUS. *Die kommunistische Ideologie*. Bonn: Bundeszentrale für Heimatdienst, 1956. 75p.
963. KÖHLER, HANS. *Das Menschenbild des dialektischen Materialismus*. München: A. Pustet, 1957. 37p.
964. KULTSCHYTSKYJ, ALEXANDER VON. *Die marxistisch-sowjetische Konzeption des Menschen im Lichte der westlichen Psychologie*. München: Institut zur Erforschung der UdSSR, 1956. 112p.
965. LANGE, MARIANNE. *Bürgerliches und marxistisch-leninistisches Menschenbild*. Berlin: Dietz, 1961. 69p.
966. THIER, ERICH. *Das Menschenbild des jungen Marx*. Göttingen: Vandenhoeck & Ruprecht, 1957. 77p.
967. TILLICH, PAUL. *Der Mensch im Christentum und im Marxismus*. Stuttgart: Ring Verlag, 1952. 18p.

See also: 7, 8, 70, 174, 279, 330, 343, 379, 428, 500, 536, 538, 588, 598, 639, 678, 706, 801, 971, 973, 978, 981, 983, 986, 991, 1040, 1139, 1200, 1239, 1275, 1293, 1296, 1316, 1417.

20 ————————————— ALIENATION

The discussion of the Marxist view of alienation has centered around the study of Marx's early work. 969, 978, 988, and 991 are examinations of the philosophical ideas of the young Marx. 969 is especially helpful in laying bare the sources of Marx's ideas about the condition of the alienated producer. 984 is an able discussion of the development of Marx's thought about human alienation, revolution, and emancipation. 979 relates Marx's concept of estrangement to Hegel's; 975 is an exceptionally erudite dissertation on the history of the concepts of the alienation of labor and the alienation of language from Spinoza through Hegel and Marx to current existentialism. 977 argues for the usefulness of the concept of alienation without, however, making much headway in its analysis.

971 is a clear and forceful explication of the central ideas of Marx. It devotes special attention to the relation of Marx's early work to his more mature writings; even though Tucker's psychological interpretation of alienation is inadequate, his book is excellent as an introduction. 983 is a weak critique of 944 and 971. 973 argues for the view that the mature Marx is substantially different from the Marx of the early manuscripts and describes Lukács' role in reintroducing the concept of alienation into Marxist philosophy. 987 is an important study of Marx and Lukács, with special reference to the notion of reification. 980 is a good short treatment of Marx. 972 will not go down in history as the last or the best evaluation of Lukács' work, although there is none better today. It is, in any case, too early to give a final assessment of Lukács: his book on the ontology of labor—his most important work in his own opinion—is not as yet completed. 974 is a cumbersome examination

of alienation, purpose, and the division of labor in Marx. 970 is an interpretation based on Marx and Tönnies. 990 is a major Soviet work in translation.

A study of the works listed below should make clear that Marx's theory of alienation and its relation to the views of other philosophers have been studied in some detail. The most glaring shortage in the literature is of works devoted to mapping the logical features of the concept(s) of alienation in preparation for assessing their philosophical usefulness. This task will have to be accomplished in a context wider than that of Marxism. Its completion, however, will make a substantial contribution to our understanding and evaluation of the thought of the young Marx.

968. ADAMS, HENRY P. *Karl Marx in His Earlier Writings.* London: Allen and Unwin, 1940. 221p.
969. CORNU, AUGUSTE. *The Origins of Marxian Thought.* Springfield, Ill.: C. C. Thomas, 1957. 128p.
970. PAPPEMHEIM, FRITZ. *The Alienation of Modern Man.* New York: Monthly Review Press, 1959. 189p.
971. TUCKER, ROBERT C. *Philosophy and Myth in Karl Marx.* Cambridge: Cambridge University Press, 1961. 263p.
972. ZITTA, VICTOR. *Georg Lukács' Marxism: Alienation, Dialectics, Revolution.* The Hague: Martinus Nijhoff, 1964. 305p.

973. BELL, DANIEL. "The 'Rediscovery' of Alienation: Some Notes along the Quest for the Historical Marx," *Journal of Philosophy* 56 (1959), 933–52.
974. BRAYBROOKE, DAVID. "Diagnosis and Remedy in Marx's Doctrine of Alienation," *Social Research* 25 (1958), 325–45.
975. FRANKLIN, MITCHELL. "On Hegel's Theory of Alienation and its Historic Force," *Tulane Studies in Philosophy* 9 (1960), 50–100.
976. HODGES, DONALD C. "The Young Marx—A Reappraisal," *Philosophy and Phenomenological Research* 27 (1966), 216–29.
977. HOROWITZ, IRVING L. "On Alienation and the Social Order," *Philosophy and Phenomenological Research* 27 (1966), 230–37.
978. LANGSLET, LARS R. "Young Marx and Alienation in Western Debate," *Inquiry* 6 (1963), 3–17.
979. LÖWITH, KARL. "Man's Self-Alienation in the Early Writings

of Marx," *Social Research* 21 (1954), 204–30.

980. O'NEILL, JOHN. "The Concept of Estrangement in the Early and Later Writings of Karl Marx," *Philosophy and Phenomenological Research* 25 (1964), 64–84.

981. ———. "Marxism and Mythology," *Ethics* 77 (1966), 38–49.

982. PARSONS, HOWARD L. "The Prophetic Mission of Karl Marx," *The Journal of Religion* 44 (1964), 52–72.

983. SCHAFF, ADAM. "Review of Erich Fromm, *Marx's Concept of Man* and Robert C. Tucker, *Philosophy and Myth in Karl Marx*," *History and Theory* 2 (1963), 307–18.

984. VOEGELIN, ERIC. "Formation of the Marxian Revolutionary Idea," *The Review of Politics* 12 (1950), 275–302.

985. NAVILLE, PIERRE. *De l'aliénation à la jouissance*. Paris: M. Rivière, 1957. 514p.

986. BLANCHARD, YVON. "Note sur le caractère philosophique de la pensée de Karl Marx," *Dialogue* 1 (1962), 153–62.

987. GOLDMANN, LUCIEN. "La Réification," *Les Temps Moderne* 14 (1959), 1433–74.

988. GURVITCH, GEORGES. "La sociologie du jeune Marx," *Cahiers Internationaux de Sociologie* 4 (1948), 3–47.

989. CORNU, AUGUSTE. *Karl Marx, die ökonomisch-philosophischen Manuskripte*. Berlin: Akademie-Verlag, 1955. 54p.

990. OIZERMAN, T. I. *Entfremdung als historische Kategorie*. Berlin: Dietz, 1964.

991. POPITZ, HEINRICH. *Der entfremdete Mensch; Zeitkritik und Geschichtphilosophie des jungen Marx*. Basel: Verlag für Recht und Gesellschaft, 1953. 172p.

See also: 7, 8, 75, 330, 343, 364, 397, 910, 944, 956, 961, 966, 1139.

2I ——————— THE INDIVIDUAL IN SOCIETY AND IN HISTORY

This section encompasses both the issue of the individual's relation to his society and that of the role of the individual in initiating or controlling historical processes. As before, few books are devoted to these subjects alone; most of the relevant works will be found listed in the "See also" column.

995 contends that individual freedom and fulfillment are only possible in a classless society. The author's pleasant style and his tone of assurance almost succeed in concealing the scarcity of arguments in support of his claim. 998 contrasts Mill's view of the primacy of the individual with Marx's opinion that the individual can only fulfill himself by membership in a collectivity.

999 is a major study of the historical materialist view of the relation of man in his singularity to the irresistible trends of history. The same problem is discussed in 996; 997 concludes that even such a great man as Lenin could only guide historical movements, not make them. 922 and 1000 are useful studies, written from divergent points of view, of the role of man and the great man in society.

992. HOOK, SIDNEY. *The Hero in History*. Boston: Beacon Press, 1955. 254p.
993. *The Individual and Communism*. Moscow: Novosti Press Agency Publishing House, 1966. 114p.
994. KAMMARI, M. D. *Socialism and the Individual*. Moscow: Foreign Languages Publishing House, 1952. 99p.

995. LEWIS, JOHN. *Socialism and the Individual*. New York: International Publishers, 1961. 125p.
996. PLEKHANOV, GEORGII V. *The Role of the Individual in History*. New York: International Publishers, 1940. 62p.

997. PRICE, M. PHILLIPS. "Lenin," *The Labour Monthly* 6 (1959), 527–30.
998. WARD, JOHN W. "Mill, Marx, and Modern Individualism," *Virginia Quarterly Review* 35 (1959), 527–39.

999. KAMMARI, M. D. *Der Marxismus-Leninismus über die Rolle der Persönlichkeit in der Geschichte*. Berlin: Dietz, 1955. 558p.
1000. MÁCHA, KAREL. *Individuum und Gesellschaft*. Berlin: Deutscher Verlag der Wissenschaften, 1964. 321p.

See also: 14, 75, 174, 327, 343, 377, 641, 656, 691, 699, 701, 714, 723, 729, 736, 772, 835, 841, 848, 857, 876, 905, 945, 955, 956, 1009, 1022, 1040, 1287, 1301, 1314, 1405.

22 ———————————— FREEDOM

The philosophical study of the dialectical materialist view of freedom has not been a particularly careful one. For the most part, writers have not made the necessary distinctions between the logical, metaphysical, psychological, and political issues that are all referred to, indifferently, by the phrase "the problem of freedom." Fired by a sort of righteous indignation, some thinkers have even forgotten to distinguish between the theory of Marxism-Leninism and the actual circumstances that prevail in the Soviet Union; such current practice is taken by them to reveal "the real" Marxist-Leninist theory or to refute the generally avowed one. A good example of the former muddle is 1008, in which the author fails to make the central distinction between the freedom of the will and political liberty. I have tried to exclude all works that manifest the latter confusion between theory and practice.

The most serious Marxist attempt to deal with the diverse notions of freedom is 1011. Aptheker (1002) writes as an apologist, but without the philosophical acumen necessary to defend his view. 1004 and 1005 deserve study even though both abound in unsupported general statements. 1010 contains a neat summary; its philosophical contribution, however, is limited. 1003 and 1006 contain examinations of the historical materialist view of political freedom. 1001 is a useful background work on the varieties of the idea of freedom. 1009 contrasts the "democratic" theory of Marx with the totalitarian conviction and practice of both Lenin and Stalin.

1001. ADLER, MORTIMER. *The Idea of Freedom.* Garden City, N.Y.: Doubleday, 1958–61. 2 vols.

1002. APTHEKER, HERBERT. *On the Nature of Freedom: The Marxist View.* New York: New Century Publishers, 1960. 32p.

1003. DEWEY, JOHN. *Freedom and Culture.* New York: Putnam's, 1939. 176p.

1004. DUNAEVSKAIA, RAIA. *Marxism and Freedom.* New York: Bookman Associates, 1958. 384p.

1005. HEIMANN, EDUARD. *Freedom and Order.* New York: Scribner, 1947. 344p.

1006. RUSSELL, BERTRAND. *Freedom versus Organization, 1814–1914.* New York: Norton, 1934. 471p.

1007. ADDIS, LAIRD. "Freedom and the Marxist Philosophy of History," *Philosophy of Science* 33 (1966), 101–17.

1008. CRAMER, FREDERICK H. "Definitions of Freedom: Marx vs. Schopenhauer," *Forum* 112 (1949), 193–99.

1009. SOWELL, THOMAS. "Karl Marx and the Freedom of the Individual," *Ethics* 73 (1963), 119–25.

1010. FETSCHER, IRING. *Die Freiheit im Lichte des Marxismus-Leninismus.* Bonn: Bundeszentrale für Heimatdienst, 1959. 78p.

1011. GARAUDY, ROGER. *Die Freiheit als philosophische und historische Kategorie*. Berlin: Dietz, 1959. 555p.

See also: 174, 206, 327, 352, 489, 522, 723, 729, 770, 835, 841, 846, 857, 858, 861, 864, 876, 953, 1067, 1239, 1370.

23 ———————— THE SECOND STAGE
OF COMMUNIST SOCIETY

The future utopia toward which, Marxists believe, history inevitably moves has never been described in adequate detail. Marx, Engels, and Lenin spoke only in guarded generalities about this distant condition of human society; their followers spend many more pages praising the future in store for us than describing it. Perhaps it is indeed impossible to do more than present a schematic sketch of the future. But I cannot help thinking that if a group of men are ready to sacrifice their own and others' welfare—even lives —for an ideal, it would be reasonable for them to have a clear and accurate idea of the good they wish to achieve as well as of its feasibility.

In fact, unfortunately, the most we can obtain from historical materialists is a general description of the road to be followed toward communism, as in 1013, with some general hints as to what we may hope to see once we get there. 1015 informs us that the path to the second stage of Communist society is the path to happiness. This would be a helpful piece of information, if only Rosental gave us some idea of what happiness might be. 1012 and 1014 are more sober assessments; 1016 argues that the second stage of Communist society can never be achieved. 1017 maintains that if the dialectic is taken seriously, communism cannot be the final stage in the development of human society. 1018 is the latest analysis of some utopian ideas of Marxist-Leninists.

1012. HUNT, ROBERT N. C. *Socialism into Communism*. Oxford: St. Antony's College, 1956. 20p.
1013. IUDIN, PAVAL F. *From Socialism to Communism*. Moscow: Progress Publishers, 1964. 110p.
1014. LAQUEUR, WALTER Z., and LABEDZ, LEOPOLD. *The Future of Communist Society*. New York: Praeger, 1962. 196p.
1015. ROSENTAL, EDUARD M. *These Are Our Ideals*. New York: Crosscurrents Press, 1962. 31p.

1016. BOBER, M. M. "Discussion," *American Economics Review* 39 (1949), 40–44.
1017. REEKIE, A. G. "End of Communism," *Hibbert Journal* 46 (1948), 260–62.
1018. ULAM, ADAM. "Socialism and Utopia," *Daedelus* 94 (1965), 382–400.

1019. BLOCH, ERNST. *Das Prinzip Hoffnung*. Berlin: Aufbau-Verlag, 1954. 2 vols.

See also: 18, 48, 174, 644, 666, 668, 722, 756, 766, 874, 953, 974, 995, 1301, 1432.

24 ——————— MARXIST ETHICS

There are many discussions of the morals of Marxists and relatively few of the ethics of Marxism. The systematic ethical genius of a Sidgwick or a G. E. Moore has never been directed upon the ethical views tacit or explicit in the classic expositions of historical materialism. However, Kamenka's recent book (1022) goes a long way toward uncovering some of the ethical assumptions of Marxism. 1035 and 1037 concentrate on the analysis of limited aspects of Marxist ethics; 1036 and 1039 serve, at best, as general introductions. 1046 is an interesting comparison of Marxist and Christian ethics, but it is without philosophical depth. 1026 contains relevant remarks by an outstanding Protestant theologian.

Among expositions and defenses of the Marxist view of ethics, 949 stands out as an ambitious and promising effort. The weakness of the author's analytic skill is one of the main sources of the book's failure. Selsam's 1031 is probably his best work (it is certainly better than his 1030), but not good enough to make a permanent contribution. 1025 is the attempt of a leading British Marxist to bring about a *rapprochement* of historical materialism and some current Western thought on such issues as human rights, democracy, and ultimate values. 1023 raises grave ethical problems about historical responsibility. In 1040 Marković, an important Yugoslav philosopher, stresses the humanistic element in Marx perhaps too much to the exclusion of other factors. 1043 and 1049 are important German translations from the Russian.

I have included only a few works that deal with casuistry and practical moral issues. The brief report that constitutes 1028 is an outcome of the author's recent visit to the Soviet Union. 1033 is a polemic against the objectives, methods, and morality of Communists. 1038 is a sober study of some recent developments in the Soviet Union. 1041 and 1047 are general accounts of the moral principles of Marxist-Leninists.

1020. ASH, WILLIAM. *Marxism and Moral Concepts*. New York: Monthly Review Press, 1964. 204p.
1021. BARTON, WILLIAM E. *The Moral Challenge of Communism: Some Ethical Aspects of Marxist-Leninist Society*. London: Friends Home Service Committee, 1966. 105p.
1022. KAMENKA, EUGENE. *The Ethical Foundations of Marxism*. New York: Praeger, 1962. 208p.
1023. KAUTSKY, KARL. *Ethics and the Materialist Conception of History*. Chicago: Kerr, 1907. 206p.
1024. KROPOTKIN, PETER A. *Ethics, Origin and Development*. New York: Dial Press, 1924. 349p.

1025. LEWIS, JOHN. *Marxism and the Open Mind*. London: Routledge and Kegan Paul, 1957. 222p.

1026. NIEBUHR, REINHOLD. *Moral Man and Immoral Society*. New York: Scribner, 1933. 284p.

1027. NIVISON, DAVID S. *Communist Ethics and Chinese Tradition*. Cambridge, Mass.: M.I.T. Press, 1954. 83p.

1028. PARSONS, HOWARD L. *Ethics in the Soviet Union Today*. New York: American Institute for Marxist Studies, 1965. 25p.

1029. PETRAZHITSKII, LEV I. *Law and Morality*. Cambridge, Mass.: Harvard University Press, 1955. 335p.

1030. SELSAM, HOWARD. *Ethics and Progress*. New York: International Publishers, 1965. 128p.

1031. ———. *Socialism and Ethics*. New York: International Publishers, 1943. 223p.

1032. TROTSKII, LEV D. *Their Morals and Ours*. New York: Pioneer Publishers, 1942. 48p.

1033. BROWN, W. J. "From Marx to Marriage," *The Spectator* 180 (1948), 367–68.

1034. GIDDINGS, FRANKLIN H. "The Ethics of Socialism," *Ethics* 1 (1890–91), 239–43.

1035. HODGES, DONALD C. "Historical Materialism in Ethics," *Philosophy and Phenomenological Research* 23 (1962–63), 1–22.

1036. HUNT, ROBERT N. C. "The Ethics of Marxism," *Nineteenth Century and After* 145 (1949), 108–17.

1037. KAMENKA, EUGENE. "The Primitive Ethic of Karl Marx," *Australasian Journal of Philosophy* 35 (1957), 75–96.

1038. KLINE, GEORGE L. " 'Socialist Legality' and Communist Ethics," *Natural Law Forum* 8 (1963), 21–34.

1039. LAIRD, JOHN. "The Ethics of Communism," *Journal of Philosophical Studies* 3 (1928), 198–212.

1040. MARKOVIĆ, MIHAILO. "Marxist Humanism and Ethics," *Inquiry* 6 (1963), 18–34.

1041. GARAUDY, ROGER. *Le communisme et la morale*. Paris: Éditions sociales, 1945. 127p.

1042. ———. *Qu'est-ce que la morale marxiste?* Paris: Éditions sociales, 1963. 232p.

1043. ARKHANGEL'SKII, LEONID M. *Kategorien der marxistischen Ethik*. Berlin: Dietz, 1965. 310p.

1044. ASHOLT, THEODOR. *Marxismus und Ethik.* Giessen: 1928. 91p.
1045. BOECK, HANS. *Zur marxistischen Ethik und sozialistischen Moral.* Berlin: Akademie-Verlag, 1959. 168p.
1046. FUCHS, EMIL. *Christliche und marxistische Ethik.* Leipzig: Koehler & Amelang, 1956.
1047. KAREVA, MARIIA P. *Recht und Moral in der sozialistischen Gesellschaft.* Berlin: Kultur und Fortschritt, 1954. 182p.
1048. KLENNER, H. *Der Marxismus-Leninismus über das Wesen des Rechts.* Berlin: Deutsche Zentralverlag, 1954. 98p.
1049. SCHISCHKIN, ALEKSANDER F. *Grundlagen der marxistischen Ethik.* Berlin: Dietz, 1964. 549p.

See also: 16, 30, 207, 414, 729, 930, 1126, 1231, 1377, 1378, 1425.

25 ——— MARXIST AESTHETICS

For a systematic, exhaustive, and dull account of the aesthetics of Marxism the reader may turn to 1095. Koch's careful study (1101) is in places much more interesting, but it lacks the above volume's official sanction. One of the better introductions in English by a Marxist is 1055. 1068, 1075, and 1076 also contain useful introductory material. 1060 is the translation of a controversy among Soviet critics about the function of literature. 1078 will acquaint the reader with more recent, though essentially unchanged, Soviet thought on the subject. 1059 is a look at the nature and development of the arts from the historical materialist standpoint.

The social role of art and literature has been the storm center of many controversies over the aesthetics of Marxism. 1093 makes the important claim that there can be no single, unified Marxist-

Leninist aesthetics: Engels' and Lenin's theories of the function of literature are radically different. The unity of the views of Marx, Engels, Lenin, and Stalin is affirmed but not established in 1098. 1077 and 1106 discuss the Marxist view of the origin of literature and its use as a weapon in the class war. In 1074 the talented Marxist literary critic's attention is focused on the relation of art to the society in which it flourishes; 1105 also discusses this topic, among numerous others. 1082 defends the claim that all literature has political content. The article contains some interesting evaluations of the work of Russian and Western writers.

Problems of the Marxist-Leninist theory of socialist realism are discussed in 1065, 1084, 1088, 1091, and 1099. 1052 is a passionate denunciation of Stalin's "Literary Inquisition," with a philosophically weak account of the principles of Marxist-Leninist aesthetics. 1085 contrasts the aesthetic theory of the young Marx with the theory of art in Stalinist Russia. Both 1085 and 1067 mount attacks against Socialist realism.

In 1069 Lukács examines the reflection in literature of social unrest and the continued war of classes. In 1070 he examines the the work of Zola and Tolstoy, among others. 1073 presents a remarkable view of Shakespeare; it is of great interest despite the fact that it is neither fully substantiated nor believable. 1086 takes the indefensible view that the decline of Marxism in British and American literature was due to the fact that "the writer cannot place allegiance to party above allegiance to humanity." Hyman (1087) gives an impressive catalogue of Marxist literary critics in the United States, England, and the Soviet Union, and attributes their failure mostly to ignorance and tendentiousness. 1103 is an assessment of Marx and Engels as literary historians by one who far outshines them in that field. 1107 is a study of the work of the Soviet aesthetician A. I. Burow in the context of a brief history of the Marxist-Leninist philosophy of art.

The reader's special attention is called to 1079, 1080, and 1081. In these articles Bogdanov argues forcefully that "proletarian art" should not be limited to "social agitational themes" (1079) and that the value of poetry is not a function of its social content alone (1080). In 1081 he outlines the tasks of "proletarian criticism" and presents, among others, an interesting analysis of Hamlet. 1104 is an important work by an outstanding Soviet educator. Finkelstein's work (1056, 1057, 1058), though uneven, is insightful and provocative. Both Harap (1063) and Gorkii (1062) are worth serious study. 915, mentioned in the "See also" section, contains Plekhanov's important *Letters Without Address*.

1050. AARON, DANIEL. *Writers on the Left*. New York: Harcourt, Brace and World, 1961. 460p.

1051. EASTMAN, MAX. *Art and the Life of Action*. New York: Knopf, 1934. 226p.

1052. ———. *Artists in Uniform*. New York: Knopf, 1934. 261p.

1053. ———. *Enjoyment of Laughter*. New York: Simon and Schuster, 1936. 367p.

1054. ———. *Enjoyment of Poetry*. New York: Scribner, 1913. 224p.

1055. FINKELSTEIN, SIDNEY W. *Art and Society*. New York: International Publishers, 1947. 288p.

1056. ———. *Existentialism and Alienation in American Literature*. New York: International Publishers, 1964. 314p.

1057. ———. *How Music Expresses Ideas*. New York: International Publishers, 1952. 128p.

1058. ———. *Realism in Art*. New York: International Publishers, 1954. 190p.

1059. FISCHER, ERNST. *The Necessity of Art*. Baltimore, Md.: Penguin Books, 1964. 234p.

1060. FLORES, ANGEL, ed. *Literature and Marxism*. New York: Critics Group, 1938. 95p.

1061. FOX, RALPH W. *The Novel and the People*. New York: International Publishers, 1937. 172p.

1062. GORKIĬ, MAKSIM. *Culture and the People*. New York: International Publishers, 1939. 224p.

1063. HARAP, LOUIS. *Social Roots of the Arts*. New York: International Publishers, 1949. 192p.

1064. KEMP, HARRY. *The Left Heresy in Literature and Life*. London: Methuen, 1939. 270p.

1065. KLINGENDER, FRANCIS D. *Marxism and Modern Art; An Approach to Social Realism*. London: Lawrence & Wishart, 1943. 52p.

1066. KOZINTSEV, GRIGORIĬ M. *Shakespeare: Time and Conscience*. New York: Hill & Wang, 1966. 276p.

1067. LEHMANN-HAUPT, HELLMUT. *Art Under a Dictatorship*. New York: Oxford University Press, 1954. 277p.

1068. LIFSHITZ, MIKHAIL. *The Philosophy of Art of Karl Marx.* New York: Critics Group, 1938. 94p.

1069. LUKÁCS, GYÖRGY. *Realism in Our Time: Literature and the Class Struggle.* New York: Harper & Row, 1964. 135p.

1070. ———. *Studies in European Realism.* London: Hillway, 1950. 277p.

1071. READ, HERBERT E. *Poetry and Anarchism.* London: Faber & Faber, 1938. 126p.

1072. RÉVAI, JÓZSEF. *Lukács and Social Realism.* London: Fore Publications, 1950. 37p.

1073. SMIRNOV, A. A. *Shakespeare: A Marxist Interpretation.* New York: Critics Group, 1936. 93p.

1074. SPRIGG, CHRISTOPHER S. (CAUDWELL, CHRISTOPHER, pseud.). *Illusion and Reality.* London: Macmillan, 1937. 351p.

1075. STRACHEY, JOHN. *Literature and Dialectical Materialism.* New York: Covici, Friede, 1934. 54p.

1076. THOMSON, GEORGE D. *Marxism and Poetry.* New York: International Publishers, 1946. 71p.

1077. TROTSKII, LEV D. *Literature and Revolution.* Ann Arbor, Mich.: University of Michigan Press, 1960. 262p.

1078. ZHDANOV, ANDREI A. *Essays on Literature, Philosophy, and Music.* New York: International Publishers, 1950. 96p.

1079. BOGDANOV, ALEKSANDR A. "The Criticism of Proletarian Art," *The Labour Monthly* 5 (1923), 344–56.

1080. ———. "Proletarian Poetry," *The Labour Monthly* 4 (1923), 275–85, 357–62.

1081. ———. "The Workers' Artistic Inheritance," *The Labour Monthly* 6 (1924), 549–56.

1082. FADEEV, ALEKSANDR A. "The Tasks of Literary Criticism," *The American Review on the Soviet Union* 11 (1948), 30–59.

1083. FIZER, JOHN. "The Problem of the Unconscious in the Creative Process as Treated by Soviet Aesthetics," *The Journal of Aesthetics and Art Criticism* 21 (1963), 399–406.

1084. FOLEJEWSKI, ZBIGNIEW. "Frustrations of Socialist Realism," *The Journal of Aesthetics and Art Criticism* 14 (1956), 485–88.

1085. GELPI, DONALD. "Art and Communism," *Thought* 38 (1963), 39–55.

1086. GLICKSBERG, CHARLES I. "The Decline of Literary Marxism," *The Antioch Review* 1 (1941), 452–62.

1087. HYMAN, STANLEY E. "The Marxist Criticism of Literature,"
    The Antioch Review 7 (1947), 541–68.
1088. KOPECZI, B. "New Problems of Socialist Realism," *The New
    Hungarian Quarterly* 6 (1965), 75–80.
1089. MASLOW, VERA. "George Lukács and the Unconscious," *The
    Journal of Aesthetics and Art Criticism* 22 (1964), 465–70.
1090. MUNRO, THOMAS. "The Marxist Theory of Art History:
    Socio-Economic Determinism and the Dialectical Process,"
    The Journal of Aesthetics and Art Criticism 18 (1960),
    430–45.
1091. RIESER, MAX. "The Aesthetic Theory of Social Realism,"
    The Journal of Aesthetics and Art Criticism 16 (1957),
    237–48.
1092. ———. "Russian Aesthetics Today and Their Historical
    Background," *The Journal of Aesthetics and Art Criticism*
    22 (1963), 47–53.
1093. STEINER, GEORGE. "Marxism and the Literary Critic," *En-
    counter* 11 (1958), 33–43.
1094. WILSON, EDMUND. "The Literary Class War," *The New Re-
    public* 70 (1932), 321–23, 347–49.

1095. AKADEMIIA NAUK SSSR. *Grundlagen der marxistisch-lenin-
    istischen Ästhetik.* Berlin: Dietz, 1962. 726p.
1096. BUROW, A. J. *Das ästhetische Wesen der Kunst.* Berlin:
    Dietz, 1958. 330p.
1097. JUST, GUSTAV. *Karl Marx zu Fragen der Kunst und Literatur.*
    Berlin: Aufbau-Verlag, 1953. 71p.
1098. ———. *Marx, Engels, Lenin und Stalin über Kunst und Li-
    teratur.* Berlin: Dietz, 1953. 88p.
1099. KEMENOV, V. S. *Über den objektiven Charakter der Gesetze
    der realistischen Kunst.* Berlin: Dietz, 1955. 63p.
1100. KOCH, HANS. *Franz Mehrings Beitrag zur marxistischen Li-
    teraturtheorie.* Berlin: Dietz, 1959. 440p.
1101. ———. *Marxismus und Ästhetik.* Berlin: Dietz, 1961. 627p.
1102. LUKÁCS, GYÖRGY. *Beiträge zur Geschichte der Ästhetik.*
    Berlin: Aufbau-Verlag, 1954. 438p.
1103. ———. *Karl Marx und Friedrich Engels als Literaturhistor-
    iker.* Berlin: Aufbau-Verlag, 1948. 244p.
1104. LUNACHARSKII, ANATOLII V. *Die Revolution und die Kunst.*
    Dresden: VEB Verlag der Kunst, 1962. 250p.
1105. PLEKHANOV, GEORGII V. *Kunst und Literatur.* Berlin: Dietz,
    1955. 1034p.

1106. RÜHLE, JÜRGEN. *Literatur und Revolution*. Köln: Kiepen-
heuer & Witsch, 1960. 610p.

1107. OELMÜLLER, WILLI. "Neue Tendenzen und Diskussionen
der marxistischen Aesthetik," *Philosophische Rundschau*
9 (1962). 181–203.

See also: 22, 591, 740, 915, 922, 1284, 1446, 1507, 1528.

26 —— MARXIST PHILOSOPHY
OF LAW

1118 includes some important essays by Russian thinkers on
the philosophical foundations of Soviet ideas about law and state.
1116 contains essential materials for the student. 1114 is the best
available critical examination of the Marxist-Leninist philosophy of
law. It is written without much sympathy, but it does make some
valid points.

1117 and 1120 are too cryptic to be of much philosophical value.
1110 contains too much empirical matter and too little of the conceptual clarity that would give it enduring philosophical value.
1119 is a Marxist critique of some of the fundamental concepts of
law. 1112 gives a short section to Marx—nowhere near enough to
do justice to his ideas on legal theory.

I have included 1108, 1109, and 1111 to make it possible for the
reader to gain firsthand acquaintance with Soviet law. It is hoped
that these books might help him tie abstract discussions of the
philosophy of law to a relatively concrete body of statutes. The
statutes, in conjunction with the official decrees, statements, and
documents contained in 1115, might, in turn, yield some insight

into the philosophical principles that presumably inspired their formulation and enactment.

1108. ACADEMY OF SCIENCES OF THE USSR. INSTITUTE OF STATE AND LAW. *Fundamentals of Soviet Law.* P. S. Romashkin, ed. Moscow: Foreign Languages Publishing House, n.d. 517p.

1109. ———. *International Law.* Moscow: Foreign Languages Publishing House, n.d. 477p.

1110. BERMAN, HAROLD J. *Justice in Russia; An Interpretation of Soviet Law.* Cambridge, Mass.: Harvard University Press, 1950. 322p.

1111. DENISOV, A., and KIRICHENKO, M. *Soviet State Law.* Moscow: Foreign Languages Publishing House, 1960. 459p.

1112. FRIEDMANN, W. *Legal Theory.* London: Stevens, 1960. 564p.

1113. HAZARD, JOHN. *Law and Social Change in the USSR.* Toronto: Carswell Co., 1953. 310p.

1114. KELSEN, HANS. *The Communist Theory of Law.* New York: Praeger, 1955. 203p.

1115. MEISEL, JAMES H., and KOZERA, EDWARD S., eds. *Materials for the Study of the Soviet System.* Ann Arbor, Mich.: G. Wahr, 1950. 495p.

1116. *Soviet Legal Philosophy.* Cambridge, Mass.: Harvard University Press, 1951. 465p.

1117. TIMASHEFF, NICHOLAS S. *The Crisis in the Marxian Theory of Law.* New York: New York University School of Law, 1939. 13p.

1118. VYSHINSKII, ANDREI I., ed. *The Law of the Soviet State.* New York: Macmillan, 1948. 749p.

1119. PASHUKANIS, EVGENII B. *Allgemeine Rechtslehre und Marxismus.* Wien-Berlin: Verlag für Literatur und Politik, 1929. 202p.

1120. RAPPOPORT, ANATOL. *Die marxistische Rechtsauffassung.* Riga: Selbstverlag, 1927. 54p.

See also: 48, 414, 646, 1029, 1038, 1047.

27 —— MARXISM AND RELIGION

Marxists have, on the whole, had very little to say about religion. This, however, is not at all surprising, if one considers their view of its nature. For the Marxist-Leninist, theology, of course, is of no interest; religion is a subject fit for psychological and sociological, but not for philosophical investigation. He pays virtually no attention to the attempts of theologians to criticize his views; he establishes communication with them almost exclusively when this assures him some tactical advantage. It is, accordingly, not at all remarkable that the best available historical materialist treatment of religion is still the Marx-Engels volume of selections (23). 1174 and 1184 deal with some of the same topics, although not with the same freshness and vigor. 1135 gives some new insights into the social basis of Christianity. 1138 is a confused attempt to synthesize some of the central ideas of Marx and Freud. 1125 contains a very remarkable set of reflections on the symbolic truth of Christianity and the literal truth of Marxism-Leninism by a defrocked Episcopal bishop.

In contrast to the Marxist-Leninist lack of interest, the reaction of theologians and Christian laymen to Marxism has been overwhelming. Unfortunately, the philosophical quality of the religious critiques has not kept up with their number. As a result, we see an abundance of such theoretically weak volumes as 1130, 1147, 1181, and 1187. 1128, 1145, 1150, and 1180 are philosophically sounder, but none is a sustained, major analysis. 1140 is a group of studies by Anglicans; 1185 and 1186 are unconvincing attacks on Marxist-Leninist atheism. 1126 is a critique of the Marxist ethic, and 1139 is a Christian's view of the young Marx's philosophical position. Tillich's generous sympathies allow him to view Marx as of continued relevance (1171). 1161 contends that historical materialists fail to distinguish between personal and organized religion, and between the realms of faith and knowledge.

Roman Catholic critiques of Marxism-Leninism range from the insubstantial 1146 to the serious and useful 1142. Pope Pius' 1127 is of significance as an official statement of position; since it is not designed to convince or persuade, it contains no philosophical arguments. For introductory comparisons of Marxism and Christianity the reader may consult 1121, 1131, 1133, 1141, 1144, and 1176. 1166 concludes that both dialectical and historical materialism conflict with basic Christian tenets. 1168 is an attack on the inadequate view of religion and morality expressed in *The Communist Manifesto*. 1122 is a study of the proper attitude of Christians to social need and political turmoil. The same issues are handled, among others, in 1137. 1123 advocates the solution of world problems by "Vedantic approach"; the author of 1149 is firmly convinced that Buddhist "scientific doctrines" can answer any challenge. In 1152 Bogdanov argues that the proletariat should appropriate all the positive elements of religion and non-proletarian art.

Some thinkers are of the opinion that to call dialectical and historical materialism a religion is to gain an important insight into its nature or, better yet, to present a powerful argument against it. The authors of 1169 and 1178 appear to hold this view; 1159 goes so far as to call Marxism the religion of "absolute secularism." 1158 sees Marxism as the modern, secular version of Christianity; 1153 portrays it as a utopian, apocalyptic vision of human history. 1154 caricatures Marx as a messianic Jewish prophet who predicted, unsuccessfully, a social millenium. 1132, 1155, 1156, and 1170 are contributions to the new dialogue that appears to be developing between Marxists and Christians. 1163 and 1164 are sound scholarly essays.

1121. BENNETT, JOHN C. *Christianity and Communism Today.* New York: Association Press, 1960. 188p.
1122. BERDIAEV, NIKOLAI A. *Christianity and Class War.* New York: Sheed and Ward, 1934. 123p.
1123. BHATTACHARYYA, BEJOY C. *Karl Marx and Vivekananda.* Calcutta: Privately printed, 1953. 106p.

1124. BIVORT DE LA SANDÉE, JACQUES DE. *Communism and Anti-Religion*. London: Burns, Oates and Washbourne, 1938. 119p.

1125. BROWN, WILLIAM M. *Communism and Christianism*. Galion, O.: Bradford-Brown Educational Co., 1920. 251p.

1126. CAMERON, J. M. *A Scrutiny of Marxism*. London: SCM Press, 1948. 128p.

1127. CATHOLIC CHURCH. POPE PIUS XI. *Atheistic Communism*, Encyclical Letter (Divini Redemptoris). Washington, D.C.: National Catholic Welfare Conference, 1937. 54p.

1128. CUNINGGIM, MERRIMON, ed. *Christianity and Communism: An Inquiry into Relationships*. Dallas, Texas: Southern Methodist University Press, 1958. 136p.

1129. D'ARCY, MARTIN C. *Communism and Christianity*. Harmondsworth, Middlesex: Penguin Books, 1956. 190p.

1130. EVANS, DONALD. *Communist Faith and Christian Faith*. Toronto: United Church of Canada, 1964. 119p.

1131. FULTON, ROBERT B. *Original Marxism*. Boston: Christopher Publishing House, 1960. 167p.

1132. GARAUDY, ROGER. *From Anathema to Dialogue: A Marxist Challenge to the Christian Churches*. New York: Herder and Herder, 1966. 124p.

1133. HECKER, JULIUS F. *Religion and Communism*. London: Chapman & Hall, 1933. 302p.

1134. HORDERN, WILLIAM. *Christianity, Communism, and History*. Nashville, Tenn.: Abingdon Press, 1954. 174p.

1135. KAUTSKY, KARL. *Foundations of Christianity*. New York: International Publishers, 1925. 480p.

1136. LAM, ELIZABETH P. *The Place of Marx in Christian Thought*. Chicago: Privately printed, 1939. 149p.

1137. LEWIS, JOHN, ed. *Christianity and the Social Revolution*. London: V. Gollancz, 1935. 526p.

1138. LINDSAY, JACK. *The Anatomy of Spirit: An Inquiry into the Origins of Religious Emotion*. London: Methuen, 1937. 182p.

1139. MacINTYRE, ALASDAIR C. *Marxism: an Interpretation*. London: SCM Press, 1953. 126p.

1140. MacKINNON, DONALD M., ed. *Christian Faith and Communist Faith*. New York: St. Martin's Press, 1953. 260p.

1141. MacMURRAY, JOHN. *Creative Society: A Study of the Relation of Christianity to Communism*. New York: Association Press, 1936. 168p.

1142. MAURIAC, FRANÇOIS, et al. *Communism and Christians*. Westminster, Md.: Newman Press, 1949. 293p.

1143. MILLER, ALEXANDER. *The Christian Significance of Karl Marx*. New York: Macmillan, 1947. 117p.

1144. NERSOYAN, TIRAN. *A Christian Approach to Communism*. London: Muller, 1942. 103p.

1145. ROGERS, EDWARD. *A Christian Commentary on Communism*. London: Epworth Press, 1959. 223p.

1146. SHEEN, FULTON J. *Communism and the Conscience of the West*. Garden City, N.Y.: Garden City Books, 1951. 247p.

1147. SINGH, SURJIT. *Communism, Christianity, Democracy*. Richmond, Va.: John Knox Press, 1965. 127p.

1148. SPARGO, JOHN. *Marxian Socialism and Religion*. New York: B. W. Huebsch, 1915. 187p.

1149. STORY, FRANCIS. *Buddhism Answers the Marxist Challenge*. Rangoon: Burma Buddhist World Mission, 1952. 102p.

1150. WEST, CHARLES C. *Communism and the Theologians: Study of an Encounter*. Philadelphia: Westminster Press, 1965. 275p.

1151. BLAKELEY, THOMAS J. "Marxist-Leninist Scientific Atheism," *Inquiry* 9 (1966), 30–46.

1152. BOGDANOV, A. "Religion, Art and Marxism," *The Labour Monthly* 6 (1924), 189–97.

1153. BORKENAU, FRANZ. "Marx's Prophecy in the Light of History; Balance Sheet after a Century," *Commentary* 7 (1949), 430–36.

1154. BROWN, W. J. "According to St. Marx," *The Spectator* 178 (1947), 711–12.

1155. CHABAS, YVES. "Christians and Marxists," *The Christian Century* 82 (1965), 1286–88.

1156. COX, HARVEY. "To End the Communist-Christian Vendetta," *The Christian Century* 28 (1966), 1375–79.

1157. DIRSCHERL, D. A. "Karl Marx's Critique of God," *The American Benedictine Review* 16 (1965), 210–18.

1158. FULLER, EDMUND. "The Moral Challenge of the COMMUNIST MANIFESTO," *The American Scholar* 17 (1947–48), 11–17.

1159. GURIAN, WALDEMAR. "The Communist Manifesto: A Hundred Years After," *The Commonweal* 48 (1948), 516–19.

1160. HALLE, LOUIS J. "Marx's Religious Drama," *Encounter* 25 (1965), 29–37.

1161. HEDLEY, GEORGE. "Religion: What It Isn't, and Is," *Vital Speeches* 14 (1947), 148–52.
1162. JACOBSON, NOLAN P. "Marxism and Religious Naturalism," *The Journal of Religion* 29 (1949), 95–113.
1163. LIDTKE, VERNON L. "Bebel and German Social Democracy's Relation to the Christian Churches," *Journal of the History of Ideas* (1966), 245–64.
1164. LOBKOWICZ, NICHOLAS. "Karl Marx's Attitude toward Religion," *The Review of Politics* 26 (1964), 319–52.
1165. MACÍNTYRE, ALASDAIR C. "Marxists and Christians," *The Twentieth Century* 170 (1961), 28–37.
1166. MAYO, HENRY B. "Marxism and Religion," *Hibbert Journal* 51 (1953), 226–33.
1167. MEHL, ROGER. "Hope of the Marxist," *Ecumenical Review* 6 (1954), 214–28.
1168. MENCZER, BÉLA. "The Centenary of the Communist Manifesto," *The Contemporary Review* 172 (1947), 354–59.
1169. NIEBUHR, REINHOLD. "The Religion of Communism," *The Atlantic Monthly* 147 (1931), 462–70.
1170. NOVAK, MICHAEL. "The Absolute Future," *Commonweal* 85 (1967), 400–2.
1171. TILLICH, PAUL. "How Much Truth is There in Karl Marx?" *The Christian Century* 65 (1948), 906–8.

1172. DESROCHES, HENRI C. *Marxisme et religions.* Paris: Presses Universitaires de France, 1962. 125p.
1173. DUQUESNE, MARCEL. *Brèves réflexions sur l'athéisme marxiste.* Paris: P. Téqui, 1953. 126p.
1174. GARAUDY, ROGER. *L'Église, le communisme et les chrétiens.* Paris: Éditions sociales, 1939. 368p.
1175. RENNES, JACQUES. *Jésus et Marx.* Paris: L'Amité par le livre, 1949. 252p.
1176. VANCOURT, RAYMOND. *Marxisme et pensée chrétienne.* Paris: Bloud & Gay, 1948. 304p.
1177. WACKENHEIM, CHARLES. *La faillite de la religion d'après Karl Marx.* Paris: Presses Universitaires de France, 1963. 355p.

1178. BANNING, WILLEM. *Der Kommunismus als politisch-soziale Weltreligion.* Berlin: Lettner-Verlag, 1953. 298p.
1179. EHLEN, PETER. *Der Atheismus im dialektischen Materialismus.* München: A. Pustet, 1961. 228p.

1180. FALK, HEINRICH. *Kirche und Kommunismus*. Düsseldorf: Patmos-Verlag, 1956. 106p.
1181. FUCHS, EMIL. *Marxismus und Christentum*. Leipzig: Koehler & Amelang, 1952. 213p.
1182. KARISCH, RUDOLF. *Christ und Diamat: der Christ und der dialektische Materialismus*. Berlin: Morus-Verlag, 1958. 207p.
1183. ———. *Der Christ und Stalins dialektischer Materialismus*. Berlin: Morus-Verlag, 1954. 156p.
1184. KOLMAN, ERNEST. *Wissenschaft, Religion und Marxismus*. Moskau: Verlagsgenossenschaft Ausländischer Arbeiter in der UdSSR, 1935. 62p.
1185. REDING, MARCEL. *Der politische Atheismus*. Graz: Verlag Styria, 1957. 361p.
1186. ———. *Der Sinn des marxschen Atheismus*. München: A. Pustet, 1957. 30p.
1187. SENS, WALTER. *Karl Marx: Seine irreligiöse Entwicklung und anti-christliche Einstellung*. Halle: Akademie Verlag, 1935. 154p.

See also: 23, 53, 68, 950, 967, 982, 1046, 1294, 1316, 1474, 1503.

28 ——— MARXIST PHILOSOPHY OF EDUCATION

Although education is of the greatest practical importance in the attempt to build a new kind of society, the philosophy of education has not engaged to any significant extent the attention of the classics of Marxism. For this reason, the philosophical foundations of Marxist-Leninist education must be elicited from the general principles of dialectical and historical materialism, and from the scattered remarks of Marx, Engels, and Lenin. 1199 accomplishes this task with some degree of success; the book is worthy of detailed study. 1198, on the other hand, has only a limited amount of theoretical discussion. 1189 and 1190 contain essays of uneven quality; there are, however, some enlightening pieces in each.

1193 is a group of translated papers on such topics as reward and punishment in education and the roles of heredity and environment in the development of personality. 1194 is a critical examination of the Marxist-Leninist theory of education and of the way it has been put into practice in the Soviet Union. Shore's treatment lacks both depth and clarity. 1191 and 1192 are important works by a very distinguished Soviet educator; 1200 is the translation of a standard work. 1196 is an eloquent but conceptually naïve plea for attention to the principles, techniques, and results of Marxist-Leninist education. 1188 contains a selected bibliography on Soviet education.

1188. DE WITT, NICHOLAS. *Education and Professional Employment in the USSR*. Washington, D.C.: National Science Foundation, 1961. 856p.
1189. KING, EDMUND J., ed. *Communist Education*. Indianapolis, Ind.: Bobbs-Merrill, 1963. 309p.
1190. KLINE, GEORGE L., ed. *Soviet Education*. New York: Columbia University Press, 1957. 192p.
1191. MAKARENKO, ANTON S. *A Book for Parents*. Moscow: Foreign Languages Publishing House, n.d. 411p.
1192. ———. *Problems of Soviet School Education*. Moscow: Progress Publishers, 1965. 153p.
1193. REDL, HELEN G., ed. *Soviet Educators on Soviet Education*. New York: The Free Press of Glencoe, 1964. 252p.
1194. SHORE, MAURICE J. *Soviet Education: Its Psychology and Philosophy*. New York: Philosophical Library, 1947. 346p.

1195. SHORE, MAURICE J. "Marxian Thought and Education," *The Educational Forum* 5 (1940), 33–45.
1196. STURDYA, VLAD. "The Rise of the Marxian Man," *South Atlantic Quarterly* 51 (1952), 211–21.
1197. ZEPPER, J. T. "Krupskaya on Complex Themes in Soviet Education," *Comparative Education Review* 9 (1965), 33–37.

1198. POSTYSHEV, PAVEL P. *Marxistisch-leninistische Erziehung.* Moskau-Leningrad: Verlagsgenossenschaft ausländischer Arbeiter, 1933. 112p.

1199. SUCHODOLSKI, BOGDAN. *Grundlagen der marxistischen Erziehungstheorie.* Berlin: Deutsche Verlag der Wissenschaften, 1961. 566p.

1200. SUCHOMLINSKI, WASSILI. *Über die Erziehung des kommunistischen Menschen.* Berlin: VEB Verlag, 1963. 164p.

See also: 597, 612, 617, 626.

29 —— MARXIST PHILOSOPHY IN THE UNITED STATES

There has, of late, been a revival of interest in Marxist philosophy in the United States. The Society for the Philosophical Study of Dialectical Materialism has organized symposia on Marxist thought in connection with the meetings of the American Philosophical Association since 1962. The recently founded American Institute for Marxist Studies sponsors discussions and publishes pamphlets. A number of new magazines devoted, at least in part, to the examination of Marxist principles have commenced publication in the last few years. In spite of these facts, there is no major Marxist theoretician in the United States today, and no American has ever made a lasting contribution to the development or defense of dialectical and historical materialism.

The outstanding volume in this section is Rossiter's thoroughly researched and valuable 1210. Draper's works (1205, 1206) are the best available both on the theory and practice of American Marxism-Leninism. 1211 is a shorter and earlier discussion of many of the same topics. 1203 presents a Marxist analysis of American capitalism by a former leader of the Communist Party.

1209 is a philosophically poor introduction. 1215 is included as a sample of the kind of unthinking polemic that bears no results. 1201 is an interesting psychological study of what motivates people to join or leave the Communist Party. It is based on interviews with over two hundred former party members. 1214 voices alarm over the prejudiced or incompetent instruction in Marxist philosophy many United States public schools provide in response to statutory requirements. The pamphlet contains a useful bibliography.

1201. ALMOND, GABRIEL A. *The Appeals of Communism*. Princeton, N.J.: Princeton University Press, 1954. 415p.

1202. ARCHER, PETER. *Communism and the Law*. Chester Springs, Pa.: Dufour Editions, 1963. 112p.

1203. BROWDER, EARL R. *Marx and America*. New York: Duell, Sloan, and Pearce, 1958. 146p.

1204. DeLEON, DANIEL. *Marxian Science and the Colleges*. New York: New York Labor News Co., 1932. 94p.

1205. DRAPER, THEODORE. *American Communism and Soviet Russia*. New York: Viking Press, 1960. 558p.

1206. ———. *The Roots of American Communism*. New York: Viking Press, 1957. 498p.

1207. FISHER, MARGUERITE J., ed. *Communist Doctrine and the Free World*. Syracuse, N.Y.: Syracuse University Press, 1952. 284p.

1208. FOSTER, WILLIAM Z., and BROWDER, EARL R. *Technocracy and Marxism*. New York: International Publishers, 1933. 32p.

1209. OVERSTREET, HARRY A., and OVERSTREET, BONARO. *What We Must Know About Communism*. New York: Norton, 1958. 348p.

1210. ROSSITER, CLINTON. *Marxism: The View from America*. New York: Harcourt, Brace, 1960. 338p.

1211. TROTSKII, LEV D. *Marxism in the United States*. New York: Workers Party Publications, 1947. 44p.

1212. UNITED STATES DEPARTMENT OF STATE. OFFICE OF INTELLIGENCE RESEARCH AND ANALYSIS. *Research on International Communism*. Washington, D.C., 1952. 6p.

1213. WOLFE, BERTRAM. *Marx and America*. New York: John Day, 1934. 32p.

1214. ZELMAN, ANNETTE. *Teaching "About Communism" in U.S. Public Schools.* New York: Humanities, 1965. 74p.

1215. HOOVER, HERBERT. "World Experience with the Karl Marx Way of Life," *Vital Speeches* 22 (1956), 467–70.

See also: 21, 836, 1455, 1463, 1464, 1480, 1520, 1523, 1526.

30 ——— MARXIST PHILOSOPHY
IN THE SOVIET UNION

There are many acute Western observers of the Soviet philosophical scene today. There are major institutes for the study of Soviet thought and culture at Fribourg, Munich, and Berlin in Europe, and at Harvard, Columbia, and Indiana University in this country. An ever increasing flow of books and articles makes it possible even for the philosopher who reads no Russian to keep himself reasonably well-informed about the developments in dialectical and historical materialism which take place in the Soviet Union.

The classic study of philosophy in the Soviet Union is 1239. It deals with virtually every significant philosophical problem, and even if not all of Wetter's analyses are impeccable, he always has some important points to make. 1222 is a much less complete study of the history and theories of Soviet dialectical materialism. 1231 does not come up to the usual quality of Marcuse's thought. 1219 is an introductory study; 1220 places special emphasis on the critical examination of the method of Soviet philosophy. 1221 is a synopsis of a standard Soviet textbook. 1255 and 1256 discuss the evolution of Marxist-Leninist ideology in the Soviet Union, and

1265 takes stock of the situation today. Among recent books 1224 and 1240 are particularly informative and useful. Comey's work in Soviet logic (1243) promises good results.

The beginner might find it profitable to read Bocheński's 1242 first. This brief account of the general characteristics of Soviet philosophy maintains that the officially sanctioned theories consist partly of good common sense and partly of nonsense. 1246 is another introductory discussion of the development and general tenor of Soviet philosophy. It is a good summary, in spite of Kamenka's easy dismissal of Soviet philosophers as "unsophisticated" and "primitive." The article gave rise to violent replies from Soviet dialectical materialists. 1249 is yet another introductory essay; the same author's 1248 is a highly informative account of changes in Soviet intellectual climate since the death of Stalin. 1218 contains Berdyaev's evaluative essay entitled "The General Line of Soviet Philosophy."

In addition to the general works already mentioned, there are also a number of introductions especially suited for readers of minimal philosophical sophistication. 1216, 1223, 1234, 1235, 1236, 1238, and 1258 belong in this category; 1227 is among the poorest in the group. 1229 studies the Russian sources of Bolshevik ideology. 1217 is a useful glossary of Soviet philosophical terms. 1257 is only of interest to the person who can read the Russian philosophical works listed.

The first part of 1233 is an exposition and critique of Marx's thought; the second part contrasts Marxian and Soviet Marxist-Leninist theories. Other works that discuss alleged theoretical discrepancies between Marxism and Marxism-Leninism are 1259, 1260, and 1264. 1250 is a brief but pointed account of the differences between Marxism and Leninism. 1247 is a penetrating analysis of B. Petrov's (pseudonym for Boris P. Vysheslavtsev) *The Philosophic Poverty of Marxism*, in which he assails the ambiguities and inconsistencies of dialectical materialism. 1237 presents the historical and theoretical roots of the Fourth International. 1244 argues that Soviet and American philosophy are *not* equally sound. 1251 is a Soviet account of the philosophical controversy that centered around the figure of A. M. Deborin.

1216. ANTONELLI, E. *Bolshevik Russia: A Philosophical Survey.*

New York: Knopf, 1920. 307p.

1217. BALLESTREM, KARL G. *Russian Philosophical Terminology*. Dordrecht, Holland: D. Reidel, 1964. 116p.

1218. BERDIAEV, NIKOLAI A. *The End of Our Time*. London: Sheed and Ward, 1933. 258p.

1219. BLAKELEY, THOMAS J. *Soviet Philosophy*. Dordrecht, Holland: D. Reidel, 1964. 81p.

1120. ———. *Soviet Scholasticism*. Dordrecht, Holland: D. Reidel, 1961. 176p.

1221. BOCHEŃSKI, INNOCENTIUS M. *The Dogmatic Principles of Soviet Philosophy*. Dordrecht, Holland: D. Reidel, 1963. 78p.

1222. ———. *Soviet Russian Dialectical Materialism*. Dordrecht, Holland: D. Reidel, 1963. 174p.

1223. *Current Philosophical Problems: USSR* (no author). Washington, D.C.: Joint Publications Research Service, 1964. 73p.

1224. DE GEORGE, RICHARD T. *Patterns of Soviet Thought*. Ann Arbor, Mich.: University of Michigan Press, 1966. 293p.

1225. FILIPOV, ALEKSANDR. *The Concise Philosophical Dictionary: A Critical Review*. New York: Research Program of the U.S.S.R., 1953. 58p.

1226. FÜLÖP-MILLER, RENÉ. *Mind and Face of Bolshevism*. New York: Putnam's, 1927. 308p.

1227. GURIAN, WALDEMAR. *Bolshevism: An Introduction to Soviet Communism*. Notre Dame, Ind.: University of Notre Dame Press, 1963. 202p.

1128. ———. *The Future of Bolshevism*. New York: Sheed and Ward, 1936. 125p.

1229. HAIMSON, LEOPOLD H. *The Russian Marxists and the Origins of Bolshevism*. Cambridge, Mass.: Harvard University Press, 1955. 246p.

1230. KAUTSKY, KARL. *Bolshevism at a Deadlock*. London: Allen and Unwin, 1931. 193p.

1231. MARCUSE, HERBERT. *Soviet Marxism: A Critical Analysis*. New York: Columbia University Press, 1958. 271p.

1232. PETERSEN, ARNOLD. *Stalinist Conception of Marxism*. New York: New York Labor News Co., 1941. 156p.

1233. PLAMENATZ, JOHN. *German Marxism and Russian Communism*. London: Longmans, Green, 1954. 356p.

1234. POSTGATE, RAYMOND W. *The Bolshevik Theory*. London: G. Richards, 1920. 240p.

1235. SOMERVILLE, JOHN. *Soviet Philosophy; A Study of Theory and Practice.* New York: Philosophical Library, 1946. 269p.

1236. SOUVARINE, BORIS. *Stalin: A Critical Survey of Bolshevism.* New York: Longmans, Green, 1939. 690p.

1237. TROTSKII, LEV D. *Stalinism and Bolshevism.* New York: Pioneer Publishers, 1960. 27p.

1238. WEBB, SIDNEY, and BEATRICE. *Soviet Communism: A New Civilization?* New York: Scribner's, 1936. 2 vols.

1239. WETTER, GUSTAV A. *Dialectical Materialism: A Historical and Systematic Survey of Philosophy in the Soviet Union.* New York: Praeger, 1959. 609p.

1240. ———. *Soviet Ideology Today.* New York: Praeger, 1966. 334p.

1241. BLACK, CYRIL E. "Marxism, Leninism, and Soviet Communism," *World Politics* 9 (1957), 401–12.

1242. BOCHEŃSKI, INNOCENTIUS M. "On Soviet Philosophy," *The Review of Politics* 13 (1951), 344–53.

1243. COMEY, DAVID D. "Current Trends in Soviet Logic," *Inquiry* 9 (1966), 94–108.

1244. HOOK, SIDNEY. "J. H. Randall, Jr., on American and Soviet Philosophy," *Journal of Philosophy* 56 (1959), 416–19.

1245. INKELES, ALEX, and CURTISS, JOHN S. "Marxism in the USSR: The Recent Revival," *Political Science Quarterly* 61 (1946), 349–64.

1246. KAMENKA, EUGENE. "Philosophy in the Soviet Union," *Philosophy* 38 (1963), 1–10.

1247. KLINE, GEORGE L. "A Philosophical Critique of Soviet Marxism," *Review of Metaphysics* 9 (1955), 90–105.

1248. ———. "Philosophy, Ideology, and Policy in the Soviet Union," *The Review of Politics* 26 (1964), 174–90.

1249. ———. "Recent Soviet Philosophy," *The Annals of the American Academy of Political and Social Science* 303 (1956), 126–38.

1250. MEYER, ALFRED G. "Soviet Philosophy," *Current History* 25 (1953), 70–75.

1251. MIRSKY, D. S. "The Philosophical Discussion in the C.P.S.U. in 1930–31," *The Labour Monthly* 13 (1931), 649–56.

1252. MITIN, M. "Twenty-five Years of Philosophy in the USSR," *Philosophy* 19 (1944), 76–84.

1253. MÜLLER-MARKUS, SIEGFRIED. "Soviet Philosophy in Crisis," *Cross Currents* 14 (1964), 35–61.

1254. SOMERVILLE, JOHN, and RIEPE, DALE. "The American-Soviet Philosophic Conference in Mexico," *Philosophy and Phenomenological Research* 25 (1964), 122–30.

1255. CHAMBRE, HENRI. *Le marxisme en Union Soviétique*. Paris: Éditions du Seuil, 1955. 509p.

1256. COLLINET, MICHEL. *Du bolchevisme: évolution et variations du marxisme-léninisme*. Paris: Arniot-Dumont, 1957. 279p.

1257. *Bibliographie der Sowjetischen Philosophie*. Dordrecht, Holland: D. Reidel, 1959–64. I. 1959: 72p.; II. 1959: 109p.; III. 1962: 73p.; IV. 1963: 161p.; V. 1964: 143p.

1258. FALK, HEINRICH. *Die Weltanschauung des Bolschewismus*. Würzburg: Echter, 1951. 64p.

1259. FEIGLER, FRITZ. *Leninismus und Marxismus: Eine Gegenüberstellung*. München: Privately printed (?), 1950. 80p.

1260. FETSCHER, IRING. *Von Marx zur Sowjetideologie*. Wiesbaden: Hessische Landeszentrale für Heimatdienst, 1956. 51p.

1261. FILIPOV, ALEKSANDR P. *Russentum und Bolschewismus*. Stuttgart: W. Kohlhammer, 1945. 216p.

1262. FISCHL, JOHANN. *Die Weltanschauung des sowjetrussischen Materialismus*. Graz: Akademische Druck- und Verlagsanstalt, 1953. 20p.

1263. GOERDT, WILHELM. *"Fragen der Philosophie": Ein Materialbeitrag zur Erforschung der Sowjetphilosophie im Spiegel der Zeitschrift "Voprosy Filosofii" 1947–1956*. Köln: Westdeutscher Verlag, 1960. 382p.

1264. MAUTNER, WILHELM. *Der Bolschewismus*. Berlin: W. Kohlhammer, 1922. 368p.

1265. WETTER, GUSTAV A., und LEONHARD, WOLFGANG. *Sowjetideologie Heute*. Frankfurt am Main: Fischer Bücherei, 1962–63. 2 vols.

See also: 233, 354, 390, 412, 480, 494, 513, 609, 616, 622, 628, 631, 659, 695, 1078, 1083, 1092, 1095, 1107, 1116, 1409, 1413, 1416, 1416(a), 1422, 1425, 1487, 1490.

31 — PHILOSOPHY AND SOCIETY IN THE SOVIET UNION

A. Theory and Practice in the Soviet Union

The role of Marxist-Leninist philosophy in Soviet society is discussed at length in 1267, 1288, and 1291. 1280 is a detailed study of the ways in which Marxist ideology influences social change and of the ways in which ideology is, in turn, modified under the impact of concrete problems. 1286 examines the inter-action of theory and practice in the context of the structure and operations of the Soviet Communist Party. 1287 is a collection of government documents and excerpts from Soviet writers which shows the application of Marxist-Leninist principles to such issues as the emancipation of women, free love, divorce, and abortion. 1274 discusses the theory and practice of Soviet government; 1294 interprets the Soviet government as a theocracy based on the "atheistic religion" of Marxism-Leninism.

1275 examines the effect of Marxism-Leninism on the lives of Soviet citizens. 1278 and 1281 attempt a study of the attitudes and dispositions of "Soviet man"; 1279 constructs a complete character-sketch on the basis of the author's trips to the Soviet Union. 1293 presents a rambling argument designed to show that political oppression leads to psychological repression. 1296 is an insightful assessment of the character of the Marxist-Leninist. 1289 contains excellent selections designed to show the reflection of Soviet social reality in Russian literature. Hecker's impressions of life in the Soviet Union (1273) make good, light reading.

1269, 1272, and 1277 present critical assessments of Soviet society and foreign policy. 1297 examines the part played by Marxists in the development of Russian capitalism. 1290 contains a brief article on Soviet philosophy by John Somerville. 1271 is an invaluable book for the student of Russia. Its value for the philosopher is very limited. 1282 is a useful book detailing the impact of technological developments on the structure of Soviet society.

B. The Role of Marxist Philosophy in the Russian Revolution and in Soviet Society

Carr's study (1298) is an outstanding treatment of the Russian Revolution. 1308 is Wilson's exciting narrative of the interaction of philosophical principle and practical determination in the making of the Revolution. 1306 is a historically oriented study of the conditions under which Marxist thought becomes a potent force in society. Ulam's concern is with the efficacy, not the truth, of theories. 1312 argues that the historical efficacy of Marxism is in large part the result of its "anarchist" tendencies.

1299 is valuable for assessing the relative importance of the contributions of Marxist philosophy and native Russian theories and attitudes to current Soviet thought. 1310 is a study of recent books on the influence of the Russian Pan-Slavist tradition in the Soviet Union today. 1303, 1309, and 1313 include examinations of no special distinction of the relation of Marxist-Leninist philosophy to the Soviet system; 1307 is somewhat more successful. 1305 is Trotsky's critique of Stalinist theory and practice. 1304 includes valuable comparisons of the Soviet and the Chinese versions of Marxism-Leninism.

C. Marxism in Pre-Revolutionary Russia

1323 is a good history of Russian philosophy; the recently published 1317 forms an excellent complement to it by providing many of the important original texts in translation. The third volume of 1317 includes useful selections from Russian and Soviet dialectical materialists. The second volume of 1319 contains an extensive discussion of the influence of Marxism on nineteenth-century Russian philosophy. 1316 is a wordy study of the relation of Russian thought of the last century to Soviet Marxism-Leninism. Berdyaev convicts Marxism as both anti-Christian and anti-humanist. 1320 and 1322 examine populist and socialist thought; 1325 studies the complex relation of Marx to early Russian socialism. 1328 is an able history of Russian revolutionary thought. 1321 is the first volume of a projected five-volume edition of Plekhanov's selected works. 1315 is a good treatment of Plekhanov's thought; 1324 traces the development of his political views from his early advocacy of populism to his gradual acceptance of the Marxist analysis of social change.

A.   Theory and Practice in the Soviet Union

1266. BERDIAEV, NIKOLAI A. *The Russian Idea*. New York: Macmillan, 1948. 255p.
1267. BLACK, CYRIL E., ed. *The Transformation of Russian Society*. Cambridge, Mass.: Harvard University Press, 1960. 695p.
1268. DEUTSCHER, ISAAC. *Ironies of History: Essays on Contemporary Communism*. New York: Oxford University Press, 1966. 278p.
1269. EASTMAN, MAX. *The End of Socialism in Russia*. Boston: Little, Brown, 1937. 46p.
1270. ———. *Since Lenin Died*. London: The Labour Publishing Co., 1925. 158p.
1271. FISHER, HAROLD H., ed. *American Research on Russia*. Bloomington, Ind.: Indiana University Press, 1959. 240p.
1272. GOODMAN, ELLIOT R. *The Soviet Design for a World State*. New York: Columbia University Press, 1960. 512p.
1273. HECKER, JULIUS F. *Moscow Dialogues*. London: Chapman and Hall, 1933. 284p.
1274. HENDEL, SAMUEL, ed. *The Soviet Crucible*. Princeton, N. J.: Van Nostrand, 1959. 594p.
1275. INKELES, ALEX, and BAUER, RAYMOND A. *The Soviet Citizen*. Cambridge, Mass.: Harvard University Press, 1959. 533p.
1276. KAZAKEVICH, EMILY G., and KAZAKEVICH, VLADIMIR D., eds. and trans. *Political Economy in the Soviet Union*. New York: International Publishers, 1945. 48p.
1277. KENNAN, GEORGE F. *Russia and the West under Lenin and Stalin*. Boston: Little, Brown, 1961. 411p.
1278. KOSA, JOHN. *Two Generations of Soviet Man*. Chapel Hill, N.C.: University of North Carolina Press, 1962. 214p.
1279. MEHNERT, KLAUS. *Soviet Man and His World*. New York: Praeger, 1962. 310p.
1280. MOORE, BARRINGTON. *Soviet Politics: The Dilemma of*

Power. Cambridge, Mass.: Harvard University Press, 1950. 503p.

1281. NIEMEYER, GERHART, and BESHETAR, JOHN S., JR. *An Inquiry into Soviet Mentality*. New York: Praeger, 1956. 113p.

1282. PARRY, ALBERT. *The New Class Divided: Science and Technology versus Communism*. New York: Macmillan, 1966. 364p.

1283. PITTMAN, JOHN and MARGRIT. *Peaceful Co-Existence: Its Theory and Practice in the Soviet Union*. New York: International Publishers, 1964. 156p.

1284. REAVEY, GEORGE. *Soviet Literature Today*. London: L. Drummond, 1946. 190p.

1285. RUNES, DAGOBERT D. *The Soviet Impact on Society*. New York: Philosophical Library, 1953. 202p.

1286. SCHAPIRO, LEONARD B. *The Communist Party of the Soviet Union*. New York: Random House, 1960. 631p.

1287. SCHLESINGER, RUDOLF, ed. *Changing Attitudes in Soviet Russia: The Family in the U.S.S.R.* New York: Grove Press, 1949. 408p.

1288. ———. *Marx; His Time and Ours*. London: Routledge and Kegan Paul, 1950. 440p.

1289. SIMMONS, ERNEST J. *Through the Glass of Soviet Literature: Views of Russian Society*. New York: Columbia University Press, 1953. 301p.

1290. ———., ed. *USSR: A Concise Handbook*. Ithaca, N.Y.: Cornell University Press, 1947. 494p.

1291. STIPP, JOHN L., ed. *Soviet Russia Today*. New York: Harper, 1956. 270p.

1292. WALSH, WARREN B., and PRICE, ROY A. *Russia: A Handbook*. Syracuse, N.Y.: Syracuse University Press, 1947. 140p.

1293. ANISIMOV, OLEG. "The Soviet Citizen—A Profile," *The Russian Review* 10 (1951), 15–25.

1294. HEIMANN, EDUARD. "Atheistic Theocracy," *Social Research* 20 (1953), 311–31.

1295. LAFARGE, JOHN, S. J. "Communism and the Russian Mind," *Thought* 12 (1931), 196–210.

1296. ROSENBERG, HAROLD. "The Communist; his Mentality and his Morals," *Commentary* 8 (1949), 1–9.

1297. VON LAUE, THEODORE H. "Legal Marxism and the Fate of Capitalism in Russia," *Review of Politics* 18 (1956), 23–46.

B. The Role of Marxist Philosophy in the
Russian Revolution and in Soviet Society

1298. CARR, EDWARD H. *The Bolshevik Revolution, 1917–1923.*
London: Macmillan, 1950–53. 3 vols.

1299. JOINT COMMITTEE ON SLAVIC STUDIES. *Continuity and Change in Russian and Soviet Thought.* Simmons, Ernest J., ed. Cambridge, Mass.: Harvard University Press, 1955. 563p.

1300. KINDERSLEY, RICHARD. *The First Russian Revisionists.* Oxford: Clarendon Press, 1962. 260p.

1301. KONSTANTINOV, F. V. *The Role of Socialist Consciousness in the Development of Soviet Society.* Moscow: Foreign Languages Publishing House, 1950. 113p.

1302. NORMAN, DANIEL. *Marx and Soviet Reality.* London: The Batchworth Press, 1955. 72p.

1303. NOTRE DAME, INDIANA. UNIVERSITY COMMITTEE ON INTERNATIONAL RELATIONS. *The Soviet Union: Background, Ideology, Reality; A Symposium.* Gurian, Waldemar, ed. Notre Dame, Ind.: University of Notre Dame Press, 1951. 216p.

1304. TREADGOLD, DONALD W., ed. *Soviet and Chinese Communism: Similarities and Differences.* Seattle: University of Washington Press, 1966. 528p.

1305. TROTSKII, LEV D. *The Revolution Betrayed: What Is the Soviet Union and Where Is It Going?* New York: Pioneer Publishers, 1957. 308p.

1306. ULAM, ADAM B. *The Unfinished Revolution.* New York: Random House, 1960. 307p.

1307. VIGOR, PETER H. *A Guide to Marxism and its Effects on Soviet Development.* London: Faber, 1966. 253p.

1308. WILSON, EDMUND. *To the Finland Station.* New York: Harcourt, Brace, 1940. 509p.

1309. WOLFE, BERTRAM D. *Communist Totalitarianism: Keys to the Soviet System.* Boston: Beacon Press, 1961. 328p.

1310. HUDSON, G. F. "Russian or Marxist?" *Encounter* 3 (1954), 74–77.

1311. KLINE, GEORGE L. "Marx, the *Manifesto*, and the Soviet Union Today," *The Ohio University Review* 6 (1964), 63–76.

1312. ULAM, ADAM B. "The Historical Role of Marxism and the Soviet System," *World Politics* 8 (1955), 20–45.

1313. AHLBERG, RENÉ. *"Dialektische Philosophie" und Gesell-schaft in der Sowjetunion.* Berlin: In Kommission bei Harrassowitz, Wiesbaden, 1960. 135p.

1314. LEONOW, M. A. *Kritik und Selbstkritik.* Eine dialektische Gesetzmässigkeit in der Entwicklung der Sowjetgesell-schaft. Berlin: Verlag Kultur und Fortschritt, 1949. 69p.

C. Marxism in Pre-Revolutionary Russia

1315. BARON, SAMUEL H. *Plekhanov: The Father of Russian Marx-ism.* Stanford: Stanford University Press, 1963. 400p.

1316. BERDIAEV, NIKOLAI A. *The Origins of Russian Communism.* Ann Arbor, Mich.: University of Michigan Press, 1955. 191p.

1317. EDIE, JAMES M., SCANLAN, JAMES P., and ZELDIN, MARY-BARBARA, eds. *Russian Philosophy.* Chicago: Quadrangle Books, 1965. 3 vols.

1318. LOSSKII, NIKOLAI O. *History of Russian Philosophy.* New York: International Universities Press, 1951. 416p.

1319. MASARYK, THOMAS G. *The Spirit of Russia.* New York: Macmillan, 1919. 2 vols.

1320. MENDEL, ARTHUR. *Dilemmas of Progress in Tsarist Russia: Legal Marxism and Legal Populism.* Cambridge, Mass.: Harvard University Press, 1961. 310p.

1321. PLEKHANOV, GEORGII V. *Selected Philosophical Works.* Moscow: Foreign Languages Publishing House, n.d. 898p.

1322. VENTURI, FRANCO. *Roots of Revolution.* New York: Knopf, 1960. 850p.

1323. ZENKOVSKY, VASILII V. *A History of Russian Philosophy.* New York: Columbia University Press, 1953. 2 vols.

1324. BARON, SAMUEL H. "Plekhanov and the Origins of Russian Marxism," *The Russian Review* 13 (1954), 38–51.

1325. VOLIN, LAZAR. "Karl Marx and Russia," *South Atlantic Quarterly* 52 (1953), 165–79.

1326. KOTOV, V. N. *Eindringen und Verbreitung des Ideen von Karl Marx und Friedrich Engels in Russland, von den vierziger Jahren bis in die neunziger Jahre des 19. Jahrhun-derts.* Berlin: Dietz, 1956. 94p.

1327. KRAUSE, HELMUT. *Marx und Engels und das Zeitgenössische Russland.* Giessen: Im Kommissionsverlag W. Schmitz, 1958. 144p.

1328. SCHEIBERT, PETER. *Von Bakunin zu Lenin; Geschichte der russischen revolutionären Ideologien (1840–1895)*. Leiden: E. J. Brill, 1956.

See also: 166, 224, 234, 867, 887, 896, 900, 911, 928, 936, 941, 952, 1021, 1028, 1038, 1052, 1085, 1110, 1115, 1118, 1188, 1190, 1193, 1194, 1226, 1229, 1238, 1261, 1354, 1412, 1438, 1476, 1479, 1485, 1492, 1493, 1519, 1530, 1555.

32 — PHILOSOPHY AND SCIENCE IN THE SOVIET UNION

Although it contains philosophically relevant accounts of a number of sciences, this section deals primarily with the controversy centered around the theories of the geneticist Lysenko. The reason for this emphasis is that the genetics controversy is well suited to yield insight into the peculiarly Soviet forms of interaction between philosophy, science, and socio-political factors. The person who is interested in the relation of dialectical materialism to sciences or to issues in the philosophy of science not treated here may turn to Section 8 and Section 9 for additional references.

It is best to begin one's study of the genetics controversy by reading Lysenko's views as he himself explains them in 1342 and 1343. A more complete account of his views is his 1341; 1344 is an important volume by the "founder" of Soviet genetics. 1366 is the abridged translation of an article from *Pravda*. In it the Soviet philosopher Mitin discusses with unusual clarity the theoretical significance of Lysenko's researches. In 1369 a noted Soviet geneticist argues that there was no government interference in the

Lysenko controversy. The article contains interesting remarks about the relationship of dialectical materialism to physical science. 1356 is a brief and not sufficiently dispassionate account of the development of Soviet genetics from N. I. Vavilov to Trofim Lysenko. 1361 is a much more competent account of trends in Soviet biology from 1917.

1353 is an account of the important 1948 session of the Lenin Academy of Agricultural Sciences; 1352 is a stenographic account of the entire congress translated into English. Julian Huxley was one of the important figures in the stormy controversy that erupted in the West shortly after that session. Huxley's major work on the subject is 1336. His 1358, however, is a simpler and more readable version of his views. In it he argues that "the real issue" in the genetics controversy is that the scientific principle of the appeal to facts "has been overridden by ideological considerations." 1355 is a good explication of the significance of Lysenko's views and of related developments in Soviet psychology for Marxist-Leninist theory and practice. G. B. Shaw (1368) is of the opinion that Lysenko is a neo-Lamarckian vitalist, not a Darwinian materialist. 1335 and 1346 are useful summaries; 1338 and 1363 are weaker studies. 1364 contains a good bibliography of the Lysenko controversy. 1351 is the most recent publication in English on the state of Soviet genetics.

1354 and 1349 are major examinations of Marxist biology from opposing points of view: the former is by a Marxist, the latter by a critic of Soviet genetics. The concluding pages of 1347 contain comments on Marxist biology. 1337 is an outstanding account of Soviet science and its relation to Marxist-Leninist thought from 1917 to 1932. Serious students would welcome the early appearance of a second volume of Joravsky's work, to cover developments since 1932. 1331 and 1332 contain useful information; 1365 examines the relevance of materialist philosophy for cosmological thought.

1330, 1334, 1339, 1340, 1345, 1348, and 1351 are recent translations from Joint Publications Research Service. Special attention is called to Soviet work in cybernetics (1330 and 1345) and to the interesting assessment (1362) of the relationship of Soviet philosophy to developments in this relatively new science. 1329 and 1334 give the reader a fairly accurate account of the current state of the social sciences in the Soviet Union. 1340, 1350, and 1360 cover some recent developments in Soviet psychology.

1329. AKADEMIIA NAUK SSSR. *Social Sciences in the USSR.* New York: Humanities Press, 1965. 297p.

1330. ANOKHIN, P. K. *Cybernetics and the Integrative Activity of the Brain, USSR.* Washington: Joint Publications Research Service, 1966. 30p.

1331. CHRISTMAN, RUTH C. *Soviet Science; A Symposium.* Washington, D.C.: American Association for the Advancement of Science, 1952. 108p.

1332. CURRENT DIGEST OF THE SOVIET PRESS. *The Soviet Linguistic Controversy.* New York: King's Crown Press, 1951. 98p.

1333. FYFE, JAMES. *Lysenko is Right.* London: Lawrence & Wishart, 1950. 65p.

1334. GAYEVS'KYY, A. M., et al. *Historical Science and Sociological Research, USSR.* Washington: Joint Publications Research Service, 1966. 20p.

1335. HUDSON, P. S., and RICHENS, R. H. *The New Genetics in the Soviet Union.* Cambridge, England: School of Agriculture, 1946. 87p.

1336. HUXLEY, JULIAN S. *Soviet Genetics and World Science.* London: Chatto and Windus, 1949. 244p.

1337. JORAVSKY, DAVID. *Soviet Marxism and Natural Science, 1917–1932.* New York: Columbia University Press, 1961. 433p.

1338. LANGDON-DAVIES, JOHN. *Russia Puts the Clock Back; A Study of Soviet Science and Some British Scientists.* London: V. Gollancz, 1949. 160p.

1339. LOYT, T. *Philosophical Problems of Contemporary Biology, USSR.* Washington: Joint Publications Research Service, 1966. 11p.

1340. LUR'E, A. R. *Theory of Development of Higher Mental Functions in Soviet Psychology.* Washington: Joint Publications Research Service, 1966. 10p.

1341. LYSENKO, TROFIM D. *Agrobiology.* Moscow: Foreign Languages Publishing House, 1954. 636p.

1342. ———. *Heredity and its Variability.* New York: King's Crown Press, 1946. 65p.

1343. ———. *The Science of Biology Today.* New York: International Publishers, 1948. 62p.

1344. MICHURIN, IVAN V. *Selected Works.* Moscow: Foreign

Languages Publishing House, 1949. 496p.

1345. MOISEEV, V. D. *Central Ideas and Philosophical Principles of Cybernetics, USSR.* Washington: Joint Publications Research Service, 1966. 228p.

1346. MORTON, ALAN G. *Soviet Genetics.* London: Lawrence & Wishart, 1951. 174p.

1347. NORDENSKIÖLD, ERIK. *The History of Biology.* New York: Tudor, 1935. 629p.

1348. *Philosophical Speculations Concerning Life on Earth and in Outer Space, USSR.* Washington: Joint Publications Research Service, 1966. 21p.

1349. PRENANT, MARCEL. *Biology and Marxism.* New York: International Publishers, 1938. 223p.

1350. *Soviet Goals and Some Achievements in Psychology.* Washington: Joint Publications Research Service, 1966. 52p.

1351. *Symposium on Genetics, USSR.* Washington: Joint Publications Research Service, 1966. 35p.

1352. VSESOIUZNAIA AKADEMIIA SEL'SKOKHOZIAĬSTVENNYKH NAUK IMENI V. I. LENINA. *The Situation in Biological Science; Proceedings of the Lenin Academy of Agricultural Sciences of the USSR, July 31-August 7, 1948.* New York: International Publishers, 1949. 636p.

1353. ZIRKLE, CONWAY, ed. *Death of a Science in Russia.* Philadelphia: University of Pennsylvania Press, 1949. 319p.

1354. ———. *Evolution, Marxian Biology, and the Social Scene.* Philadelphia: University of Pennsylvania Press, 1959. 527p.

1355. BAUER, RAYMOND A. "The Genetics Controversy and the Psychological Sciences in the USSR," *The American Psychologist* 4 (1949), 418–21.

1356. DARLINGTON, C. D. "The Retreat from Science in Soviet Russia," *The Nineteenth Century* 141 (1947), 157–68.

1357. DUNN, LESLIE C. "Science in the U. S. S. R.," *Science* 99 (1944), 65–67.

1358. HUXLEY, JULIAN. "Soviet Genetics: the Real Issue," *Nature* 163 (1949), 935–42, 974–82.

1359. ———. Why Lysenko is Important," *The New Republic* 121 (December 5, 1949), 11–14.

1360. IVANOV, N. V. "A Soviet View of Group Therapy," *International Journal of Psychiatry* 2 (1966), 201–11.

1361. JORAVSKY, DAVID. "Soviet Marxism and Biology Before Lysenko," *Journal of the History of Ideas* 20 (1959), 85–104.

1362. KERSCHER, LEE R. "Cybernetics and Soviet Philosophy," *International Philosophical Quarterly* 6 (1966), 270–85.
1363. LANGDON-DAVIES, JOHN. "The Russian Attack on Reason," *The Fortnightly Review* 171 (1949), 308–14.
1364. LEIKIND, MORRIS C. "The Genetic Controversy in the USSR," *Journal of Heredity* 40 (1949), 203–8.
1365. MIKULAK, MAXIM W. "Soviet Cosmology and Communist Ideology," *The Scientific Monthly* 81 (1955), 167–72.
1366. MITIN, M. "Towards the Advancement of Soviet Genetics," *The American Quarterly on the Soviet Union* 2 (1940), 37–48.
1367. MÜLLER-MARKUS, SIEGFRIED. "Niels Bohr in the Darkness and Light of Soviet Philosophy," *Inquiry* 9 (1966), 73–93.
1368. SHAW, GEORGE B. "The Lysenko Muddle," *The Labour Monthly* 31 (1949), 18–20.
1369. ZHEBRAK, ANTON R. "Soviet Biology," *Science* 102 (1945), 357–58.

See also: 417, 531, 540, 542, 544, 547, 555, 563, 564, 569, 578, 582, 583, 585, 586, 588, 589, 590, 596, 597, 598, 600, 601, 603, 605, 606, 959, 1193, 1490, 1515.

33 ——— MARXIST PHILOSOPHY
IN CENTRAL
AND EASTERN EUROPE

For general assessments of the philosophical situation in the satellite countries the reader may consult 1371 and 1377. The former Hungarian Premier's 1375 is an important and interesting plea on behalf of sounder theory and revised practice in the post-Stalin era.

1370 evaluates the situation of intellectuals in Hungary; 1379 describes some recent developments in Marxist-Leninist philosophy. 1373 is a major study of Marxist philosophy and Marxist philosophers in Hungary. 1386 is a study of dialectical materialist philosophy in Yugoslavia, with special emphasis on the years from 1945 to 1959. 1384 presents additional materials on Yugoslav thought.

1383 is a brief report on post-war philosophical developments in Poland. 1372 is a major study of Polish dialectical materialism: it contains substantial critical analyses. 1385 is an account of Czech philosophy since 1945. 1380 presents the instructive history of the post-Stalin philosophical revival centered around the East German *Deutsche Zeitschrift für Philosophie*. 1378 and 1381 are insightful and informative analyses of theory and practice in Eastern Europe.

1370. Aczél, Tamás, and Méray, Tibor. *The Revolt of the Mind.* New York: Praeger, 1960. 449p.

1371. Hayward, Max. *The Ideological Consequences of October 1956.* Oxford: St. Antony's College, 1957. 20p.

1372. Jordan, Z. *Philosophy and Ideology: The Development of Philosophy and Marxism-Leninism in Poland Since the Second World War.* Dordrecht, Holland: D. Reidel, 1963. 600p.

1373. László, Ervin. *The Communist Ideology in Hungary.* Dordrecht, Holland: D. Reidel, 1966. 351p.

1374. Milosz, Czeslaw. *The Captive Mind.* New York: Knopf, 1953. 251p.

1375. Nagy, Imre. *On Communism, in Defense of the New Course.* New York: Praeger, 1957. 306p.

1376. Parsons, Howard L. *Humanistic Philosophy in Contemporary Poland and Yugoslavia.* New York: American Institute for Marxist Studies, 1966. 12p.

1377. Stillman, Edmund O. *Bitter Harvest; The Intellectual Revolt Behind the Iron Curtain.* New York: Praeger, 1959. 313p.

1378. De George, Richard T. "Morality, Ethics and East-European Marxism," *Inquiry* 9 (1966), 11–29.

1379. Hanak, Tibor. "Philosophy under Kadar," *Survey* **40** (1962), 140–48.

1380. HOROWITZ, IRVING L. "East German Marxism: Renaissance and Repression," *Dissent* 4 (1957), 393–401.
1381. LÁSZLÓ, ERVIN. "Dynamics of Ideological Change in Eastern Europe," *Inquiry* 9 (1966), 47–72.
1382. [not used]
1383. REISER, MAX. "Polish Philosophy Today," *Journal of the History of Ideas* 24 (1963), 423–32.
1384. SVENNEVIG, T. PETTER. "The Ideology of the Yugoslav Heretics," *Social Research* 27 (1960), 39–48.

1385. LOBKOWICZ, NIKOLAUS. *Marxismus-Leninismus in der CSR.* Dordrecht, Holland: D. Reidel, 1962. 268p.
1386. VRTAČIČ, A. *Einführung in den jugoslawischen Marxismus-Leninismus.* Dordrecht, Holland: D. Reidel, 1963. 208p.

See also: 475, 509, 608, 623, 626, 633, 751, 832, 867, 1089, 1404, 1405, 1484, 1505.

34 ——————————— REVISIONISM

The historically most fateful revision of Marxism was that of Eduard Bernstein, a leading German socialist at the turn of the century. Bernstein's revisionism is clearly discernible in his collected essays (1403). His 1387 includes a critique of historical materialism and revolutionary Marxism. 1389 examines the clash of Bernstein's evolutionary socialism with Marx's revolutionary ideology. 1396 brings out Bernstein's similarity to Lassalle; 1399 renders an informed and informative account of the "heresies" of Bernstein and Trotsky. The problem of the relative merits of reform and revolution is discussed in 1391, 1395, and 1401.

For a generally good collection of essays on various forms of revisionism the reader should consult 1390. 1397 and 1398 present little-known but enlightening materials; 1404 contains a number of interesting essays. 1388 is a group of passionate attacks on revisions and revisionists of Marxism. 1394 retaliates by claiming that orthodox Marxist doctrine underwent no greater changes than those at the hands of Lenin and Stalin. 1392 argues that Stalin was a revisionist of Marxist-Leninist philosophy. 1393 consists of essays by such authors as Sidney Hook, Daniel Bell, and Bertram Wolfe on a variety of topics, including revisionism. 1405 is an important book by a talented Polish philosopher who is struggling to reconcile the demands of social responsibility with those of individual conscience.

1387. BERNSTEIN, EDWARD. *Evolutionary Socialism.* New York: B. W. Huebsch, 1912. 224p.

1388. FOSTER, WILLIAM Z., and others. *Marxism-Leninism versus Revisionism.* New York: New Century Publishers, 1956. 111p.

1389. GAY, PETER. *The Dilemma of Democratic Socialism: Eduard Bernstein's Challenge to Marx.* New York: Collier Books, 1962. 348p.

1390. LABEDZ, LEOPOLD, ed. *Revisionism; Essays on the History of Marxist Ideas.* New York: Praeger, 1962. 404p.

1391. LUXEMBURG, ROSA. *Reform or Revolution.* New York: Three Arrows Press, 1937. 48p.

1392. MEHNERT, KLAUS. *Stalin versus Marx.* London: Allen and Unwin, 1952. 128p.

1393. STANKIEWICZ, W. J., ed. *Political Thought Since World War II.* New York: The Free Press of Glencoe, 1964. 464p.

1394. BAILEY, SYDNEY D. "The Revision of Marxism," *The Review of Politics* 16 (1954), 452–62.

1395. BERNARD, L. L. "Higher Criticism of Karl Marx," *Forum* 49 (1913), 202–16.

1396. KLEENE, G. A. "Bernstein vs. 'Old-school' Marxism," *Annals of the American Academy of Political and Social Science* 18 (1901), 391–419.

1397. KOHAK, ERAZIM. "T. G. Masaryk's Revision of Marxism," *Journal of the History of Ideas* 25 (1964), 519–23.

1398. MASARYK, T. G. "The Philosophical and Scientific Crisis of Contemporary Marxism," *Journal of the History of Ideas* 25 (1964), 523–42.

1399. PLAMENATZ, JOHN. "Deviations from Marxism," *Political Quarterly* 21 (1950), 40–55.

1400. STEINER, GEORGE. "Georg Lukács and His Devil's Pact," *Kenyon Review* 22 (1960), 1–18.

1401. BAUER, OTTO. *Bolschewismus oder Sozialdemokratie?* Wien: Verlag der Wiener Volksbuchhandlung, 1921. 120p.

1402. BERNSTEIN, EDUARD. *Die Voraussetzungen des Sozialismus und die Aufgaben der Sozialdemokratie.* Stuttgart: Dietz, 1899. 188p.

1403. ———. *Zur Geschichte und Theorie des Sozialismus.* Berlin & Bern: J. Edelheim, 1901. 426p.

1404. *Georg Lukács und der Revisionismus, eine Sammlung von Aufsätzen.* Berlin: Aufbau-Verlag, 1960. 338p.

1405. KOLAKOWSKI, LESZEK. *Der Mensch ohne Alternative: Von der Möglichkeit und Unmöglichkeit Marxist zu sein.* München: Piper Verlag, 1960. 284p.

1406. LUXEMBURG, ROSA. *Sozialreform oder Revolution?* Leipzig: Buchdruckerei und Leipziger Volkszeitung, 1899. 80p.

1407. RIKLI, ERIKA. *Der Revisionismus.* Zürich: H. Girsberger, 1936. 128p.

See also: 43, 174, 190, 217, 713, 738, 823, 890, 1023, 1163, 1236, 1237, 1300, 1305, 1418.

35 - ANTHOLOGIES, TEXTBOOKS, ENCYCLOPEDIAS, AND HISTORIES OF PHILOSOPHY

It is important to remember that no group of anthologized selections can take the place of the full text of a philosophical work. Similarly, the study of textbooks is no substitute for the analysis of the volumes in which the ideas of the text originated. Finally, encyclopedias and histories of philosophy should never be allowed to become an alternative to the firsthand knowledge of the classics. Despite these considerations, however, it is clear that anthologies, textbooks, encyclopedias, and histories of philosophy have their legitimate uses. Anthologies focus the student's attention on some central statements; they also simplify the comparison and contrast of divergent views. By their perspicuous structure textbooks promote clarity and order in the mind; histories of philosophy contribute intellectual context and perspective. Encyclopedia articles are frequently among the best introductions to a given subject.

1411 is an especially useful anthology because of its wide coverage. In the section on Communism it has good selections from Marx, Engels, Lenin, and Stalin. It also has passages from the Utopian Socialists and from Feuerbach. 1410 gives an exceptionally comprehensive view of Marxist-Leninist theory and practice. 1408 ranges from Plekhanov to Khrushchev, with a commentary by the editor. The selections in 1412 cover topics from political economy to the philosophy of history; they are assembled with a view to throwing light on Soviet foreign policy. 1416 and 1418 are in many respects similar; neither one is a fully successful anthology. 1419 is especially useful because it covers a wide spectrum of political philosophies. It contains selections from Fascists, National Socialists, Thomists, and exponents of representative democracy, in addition to extracts from the works of dialectical materialists.

1415 is a major Soviet textbook, consisting of a systematic presentation of the principles of Marxism-Leninism and their application in the Soviet Union and in the international Communist movement. 1416 is a translation of the Leningrad Institute of Philosophy's textbook. Lewis contributed a philosophically helpful introduction. 1409 is a systematic, well-structured work. 1423 has an excellent treatment of Marx; 1424 contains a good essay under the title of "Marxism." 1425 includes discussions of Marxist and Soviet ethics. 1428 contains a sound but cryptic treatment of Marxism. The discussion in 1429 is more extensive; 1430 is inaccurate on several points but highly readable.

1408. ANDERSON, THORNTON, ed. *Masters of Russian Marxism.* New York: Appleton-Century-Crofts, 1963. 296p.
1409. BOCHEŃSKI, INNOCENTIUS M., and NIEMEYER, GERHART, eds. *Handbook on Communism.* New York: Praeger, 1962. 686p.
1410. BURNS, EMILE. *A Handbook of Marxism.* New York: Random House, 1935. 1087p.
1411. COHEN, CARL, ed. *Communism, Fascism, and Democracy: The Theoretical Foundations.* New York: Random House, 1962. 704p.
1412. FISHER, MARGUERITE J., ed. *Communist Doctrine and the Free World.* Syracuse, N.Y.: Syracuse University Press, 1952. 284p.
1413. FLEISCHER, HELMUT, ed. *Short Handbook of Communist Ideology.* Dordrecht, Holland: D. Reidel, 1964. 97p.
1414. GARDINER, PATRICK, ed. *Theories of History.* Glencoe, Ill.: Free Press, 1959. 549p.
1415. GUEST, DAVID. *A Textbook of Dialectical Materialism.* New York: International Publishers, 1939. 107p.
1415(a). HOOK, SIDNEY, ed. *Marx and the Marxists: the Ambiguous Legacy.* Princeton, N. J.: Van Nostrand, 1955. 254p.
1416. KUUSINEN, OTTO V., and others. *Fundamentals of Marxism-Leninism.* Moscow: Foreign Languages Publishing House, 1961. 891p.

1416(a). Lewis, John, ed. *A Textbook of Marxist Philosophy.* London: V. Gollancz, 1937. 399p.
1417. Mills, C. Wright, ed. *Images of Man.* New York: G. Braziller, 1960. 534p.
1418. ———. *The Marxists.* New York: Dell, 1962. 480p.
1419. Oakeshott, Michael. *The Social and Political Doctrines of Contemporary Europe.* Cambridge, England: Cambridge University Press, 1942. 241p.
1420. Selsam, Howard, and Martel, Harry, eds. *Reader in Marxist Philosophy.* New York: International Publishers, 1963. 384p.
1421. Shirokov, Aleksandr P. *Textbook of Marxist Philosophy.* London: Camelot Press, 1937.

1422. Akademiia Nauk SSSR. *Grundlagen der marxistischen Philosophie.* Berlin: Dietz, 1960. 748p.

1423. *The Encyclopedia Britannica.* Cambridge: Cambridge University Press, 1911. Vol. 17.
1424. *Encyclopedia Britannica.* Chicago: William Benton, 1964. Vol. 14.
1425. *Encyclopedia of Morals.* New York: Philosophical Library, 1956. 682p.

1426. *Grand Larousse Encyclopédique.* Paris: Librairie Larousse, 1961. Vols. 4 and 7.

1427. *Der Grosse Brockhaus.* Leipzig: F. A. Brockhaus, 1932. Vol. 12.

1428. Copleston, Frederick, S.J. *A History of Philosophy.* London: Burns and Oates, 1963. Vol. 7.
1429. Ferm, Vergilius, ed. *A History of Philosophical Systems.* New York: The Philosophical Library, 1950. 642p.
1430. Fuller, B. A. G. *A History of Modern Philosophy.* New York: Holt, Rinehart and Winston, 1960. 618p.

See also: 1221.

36 ——————— DOCUMENTS

Although the documents and manifestos listed below have little immediate philosophical value, they are useful in the long run because of the insight they give into the close interplay of Marxist theory and practice. 1432 gives the complete texts of four Communist Manifestos from 1848 to 1961. 1433 presents an excellent selection of Marxist-Leninist writings and documents; the editor's introduction, however, is on the whole weak. Both 1434 and 1436 contain some good selections; 1435 traces the evolution of the Communist Party as reflected by official party documents.

1431. BRANDT, CONRAD, SCHWARTZ, BENJAMIN, and FAIRBANK, JOHN K. *Documentary History of Chinese Communism.* Cambridge, Mass.: Harvard University Press, 1952. 552p.
1432. *The Communist Blueprint for the Future.* New York: Dutton, 1962. 240p.
1433. DANIELS, ROBERT V., ed. *A Documentary History of Communism.* New York: Random House, 1960. 393p.
1434. HOOK, SIDNEY. *World Communism: Key Documentary Material.* Princeton, N.J.: Van Nostrand, 1962. 256p.

1435. IZARD, GEORGES. *Où va le communisme?* Paris: Éditions Bernard Grasset, 1936. 125p.

1436. FETSCHER, IRING. *Der Marxismus; Seine Geschichte in Dokumenten.* München: Piper Verlag, 1962.

See also: 1115.

37 ———————————— JOURNALS
OF SPECIAL RELEVANCE

Not all of the journals listed in this section are of equal value to the philosopher. I shall begin by listing the most important ones. 1464 and 1480 stand out as the best American journals devoted to the study of Marxist theory. They publish many articles of theoretical interest, but very few that are critical of Marxist philosophy. 1455, 1489, and 1507 contain much of significance to theorists; 1505 is especially interesting as an indicator of the philosophical ferment among Marxist-Leninists in the post-Stalin era. 1490 is an immensely valuable tool for gaining information about recent developments in Soviet thought. It is unfortunate that too many of the articles that appear in it take the form of reports instead of independent philosophical analyses. Both 1492 and 1509 carry philosophical articles; 1493 is a useful source of information about recent developments in the intellectual life of Soviet-bloc countries. 1475 and 1488 are philosophical journals which publish some important articles in English, French, and German. Finally, 1487 is a journal of great value to the philosopher who reads no Russian: it is the only journal that makes the work of Soviet philosophers readily available to American scholars.

In addition to the above publications of central importance, there are a number of limited relevance. Journals devoted to Slavic studies regularly carry articles and reviews of a philosophical nature. For this reason, the reader will find it profitable to consult 1451, 1452, 1481, 1482, and 1483 when he wishes to explore a topic that is likely to have been discussed in depth by Soviet or East European Marxist-Leninists. 1438, 1439, 1441, 1497, and 1515 publish friendly accounts of cultural developments in the Soviet

Union. 1449, 1479, 1486, 1512, and 1513 follow the Soviet social and intellectual scene; they publish relatively objective work on some philosophical topics of current interest. 1492, 1500, and 1514 are official publications of the Institute for the Study of the USSR, located at Munich. The Institute has little sympathy with dialectical materialism; unfortunately, however, not much of philosophical value emerges from its work. 1448 and 1476 are distinctly anti-Communist in tone. 1485 translates a few Soviet articles that have theoretical relevance.

1445, 1457, 1461, 1463, 1465, 1467, 1501, 1502, 1504, and 1511 are journals of Marxist orientation. In these, as in most dialectical materialist publications, there is a *mélange* of philosophy and sociology, theory and practical politics, analysis and agitation. 1471 and 1473 are on a generally higher intellectual plane. 1503 contains some materials relevant to dialectical and historical materialism and the philosophy of religion. 1446 will be of considerable value to the reader whose interest is Marxist aesthetics.

The official publications of Socialist and Communist Parties are of limited philosophical interest. In addition to their preoccupation with practical affairs, these journals also specialize in publishing articles that, though billed as about "Marxist theory," are in reality valueless propaganda pieces. Despite these facts, however, it is possible to find occasionally in them some essays that make a philosophical contribution. It is for this reason alone that I listed 1444, 1450, 1459, 1468, 1470, 1474, 1494, 1495, 1496, 1506, and 1516. 1517, the official organ of the Social-Democratic Party of Germany in the 1870's, is of special historical interest.

In the last few years there has been a great proliferation of journals devoted to the study or propagation of Marxist theories. Many of these publications are of generally poor quality and are destined for an ephemeral existence that will not outlast the enthusiasm of a single editor. However, a number of them make significant contributions by stimulating discussion and by publishing the excess or overflow work of some able scholars. 1437, 1440, 1442, 1443, 1456, 1462, 1472, 1478, 1484, and 1518 are among the more promising recent publications. 1447, 1453, 1454, 1491, and 1510, on the other hand, have already established a name for themselves; they deserve to be canvassed when some Marxist topic is carefully researched.

1437. *Alternatives.* San Diego: The Students of the Independent Left of the University of California, 1966.

1438. *American Review on the Soviet Union.* (Formerly *American Quarterly on the Soviet Union*). New York: American Russian Institute. 1938–48.

1439. *Anglo-Soviet Journal.* London: Society for Cultural Relations with the USSR. 1940——.

1440. *Arena: A Marxist Journal of Criticism and Discussion.* Greensborough Post Office, Victoria, Australia. 1964——.

1441. *Bulletin on the Soviet Union* (later *American Review on the Soviet Union*). New York: American Russian Institute. 1936–40.

1442. *Catalyst.* State University of New York at Buffalo, Buffalo, N.Y. 1965——.

1443. *Co-Existence: A Journal for the Comparative Study of Economics, Sociology and Politics in a Changing World.* Pickering, Ontario. 1964——.

1444. *The Communist Review.* Sydney, Australia: Communist Party of Australia. 1940——.

1445. *Controversy: The Monthly Socialist Forum* (later *Left*). London. 1936——.

1446. *Dialectics: A Marxist Literary Journal.* New York: Critics Group. 1937–39.

1447. *Dissent: A Quarterly of Socialist Opinion.* New York: Dissent Publishing Association. 1954——.

1448. *East Europe: A Review of East European Affairs.* New York: Free Europe Committee. 1950——.

1449. *The Eastern Quarterly.* London. 1949——.

1450. *Fourth International: English-Language Edition of the Theoretical Organ of the International Executive Committee of the Fourth International.* Paris: Pierre Frank. 1958——.

1451. *Harvard Slavic Studies.* Harvard University, Cambridge, Mass.: Department of Slavic Languages and Literature. 1953——.

1452. *Indiana Slavic Studies.* Indiana University, Bloomington, Indiana: Indiana University Publications. Russian and East European Series, 1956——.

1453. *International Review of Social History.* Amsterdam, Netherlands. 1956——.

1454. *International Socialist Journal.* Milan, Italy. 1964——.

1455. *International Socialist Review: The Marxist Theoretical Magazine of American Socialism.* New York: International Socialist Review Publishing Association. 1934——.

1456. *Left and Right: A Journal of Libertarian Thought.* Box 395, Cathedral Station, New York, N.Y. 1965——.

1457. *The Left News.* Left Book Club. London: V. Gollancz. 1936–47.

1458. *Mainstream.* New York: Masses and Mainstream, Inc. 1948——.

1459. *Marxism Today: Theoretical and Discussion Journal of the Communist Party of Great Britain.* London: Communist Party of Great Britain. 1957——.

1460. *Marxist Quarterly.* New York: American Marxist Association. 1937.

1461. *Marxist Quarterly* (supersedes *Modern Quarterly*). 1954–57.

1462. *Marxist Quarterly.* Toronto: Progress Books. 1962——.

1463. *Masses and Mainstream* (formed by the union of *New Masses* and *Mainstream*). New York. 1948——.

1464. *Modern Monthly: A Journal of Radical Opinion.* Baltimore. 1923——.

1465. *Modern Quarterly* (superseded by *Marxist Quarterly*). London. 1938–53.

1466. *The Modern Review.* New York: American Labor Conference on International Affairs. 1947–50.

1467. *Monthly Review: An Independent Socialist Magazine.* New York. 1949——.

1468. *New Essays.* Chicago: United Workers Party. 1935–43.

1469. *New Hungarian Quarterly.* Budapest: Kultura. 1960——.

1470. *New International: A Monthly Organ of Revolutionary Marxism* (superseded by *Fourth International*). New York: Communist Party of the U.S.A. 1934–40.

1471. *New Left Review* (formerly *Universities and Left Review*). London: Stuart Hall. 1957——.

1472. *New Politics: A Journal of Socialist Thought.* New York: New Politics Publishing Co. 1961——.

1473. *The New Reasoner: A Quarterly Journal of Socialist Humanism* (combined with *The Universities and Left Review* to form *The New Left Review* in 1960). Halifax, England. 1957–59.

1474. *Political Affairs: A Theoretical and Political Magazine of Scientific Socialism* (formerly *Labor Herald; Workers Monthly; The Communist*). New York: New Century Publishers, Inc. 1922——.

1475. *Praxis: A Philosophical Journal.* Zagreb, Yugoslavia: Croatian Philosophical Society. 1965——.
1476. *Problems of Communism.* Washington: Superintendent of Documents. United States Information Agency. 1952——.
1477. *Quarterly Bulletin.* London: Marx Memorial Library. Marx House. 1942——.
1478. *Root and Branch.* Berkeley, California: Root and Branch Press. 1962——.
1479. *The Russian Review: An American Quarterly Devoted to Russia Past and Present.* Hanover, N.H.: Russian Review, Inc. 1941——.
1480. *Science and Society.* New York: Science and Society, Inc. 1936——.
1481. *The Slavic and East European Journal.* Bloomington, Indiana: American Association of Teachers of Slavic and East European Languages. 1945——.
1482. *Slavic Review: American Quarterly of Soviet and East European Studies* (formerly *American Slavic and East European Review*). University of Illinois, Urbana, Ill.: American Association for the Advancement of Slavic Studies. 1941——.
1483. *Slavonic and East European Review.* University of London, London: School of Slavonic and East European Studies. 1922——.
1484. *Socialist Thought and Practice.* Belgrade, Yugoslavia: Jugoslavia Publishing House. 1961——.
1485. *Soviet Review: A Journal of Translations* (replacing *Soviet Highlights*). New York: International Arts and Sciences Press. 1960——.
1486. *Soviet Studies: A Quarterly Review of the Social and Economic Institutions of the USSR.* Department for the Study of Social and Economic Institutions of the USSR, University of Glasgow. Oxford, England: Basil Blackwell. 1949——.
1487. *Soviet Studies in Philosophy: A Journal of Translations.* New York: International Arts and Sciences Press. 1962——.
1488. *Studia Filozoficzne.* Warsaw, Poland: Instytut Filozofii i Socjologii, Polska Akademia Nauk. 1957——.
1489. *Studies in Philosophy and Social Science* (formerly *Zeitschrift für Sozialforschung*). Frankfurt am Main, Germany: Institute of Social Research. 1932——.
1490. *Studies in Soviet Thought.* University of Fribourg, Fri-

bourg, Switzerland: Sovietica Publications of the Institute of East-European Studies. 1961——.

1491. *Studies on the Left: A Journal of Research, Social Theory and Review.* Box 2121, Madison, Wisconsin. 1959——.

1492. *Studies on the Soviet Union.* Munich, Germany: Institute for the Study of the USSR. 1961——.

1493. *Survey: A Journal of Soviet and East-European Studies* (formerly *Soviet Survey*). London: Summit House. 1956——.

1494. *World Marxist Review: Problems of Peace and Socialism.* Communist and Workers' Parties. Toronto: Progress Books. 1958——.

1495. *Cahiers du Bolchévisme.* Paris: Parti Communiste Français. 1924——.

1496. *Cahiers du Communisme.* Paris: Comité Central du Parti Communiste Français. 1924——.

1497. *Études Soviétiques* (formerly *Vie soviétiques*). Paris. 1948——.

1498. *Europe.* Paris. 1946——.

1499. *Nouvelle Critique.* Paris: Jacques Arnault. 1949——.

1500. *Problèmes Soviétiques.* Munich, Germany: Institute for the Study of the USSR. 1958——.

1501. *Recherches Internationales à la Lumière du Marxisme* (supersedes *Recherches Soviétiques*). Paris. 1957——.

1502. *Recherches Soviétiques* (superseded by *Recherches Internationales à la Lumière du Marxisme*). Paris. 1956–57.

1503. *Russie et Chrétienté.* Paris: Centre d'études "Istina." 1934——.

1504. *Archiv für die Geschichte des Sozialismus und der Arbeiterbewegung* (superseded by *Zeitschrift für Sozialforschung*). Leipzig. 1910–30.

1505. *Deutsche Zeitschrift für Philosophie.* Berlin: VEB Deutscher Verlag der Wissenschaften. 1953——.

1506. *Einheit: Zeitschrift für Theorie und Praxis des wissenschaftlichen Sozialismus.* Berlin: Zentralkomitee der Sozialistischen Einheitspartei Deutschlands. 1946——.

1507. *Kunst und Literatur: Zeitschrift für Fragen der Ästhetik und Kunsttheorie.* Gesellschaft für Deutsch-Sowjetische Freundschaft. Berlin: Verlag Kultur und Fortschritt. 1953——.

1508. *Marx-Engels Archiv*. Frankfurt am Main: Institut Marksa-Engel'sa-Lenina. 1925–27.
1509. *Marxismusstudien: Studiengemeinschaft der Evangelischen Akademien*. Tübingen: J. C. B. Mohr. 1954——.
1510. *Marxistische Blätter*. Frankfurt am Main: Eberhard Meier. 1963——.
1511. *Marx-Studien: Blätter zur Theorie und Politik des wissenschaftlichen Sozialismus*. Vienna. 1904–23.
1512. *Osteuropa: Zeitschrift für Gegenwartsfragen des Ostens*. Deutsche Gesellschaft für Osteuropakunde. Stuttgart: Deutsche Verlags-Anstalt. 1952——.
1513. *Ost-Probleme*. Bad-Godesberg, Germany. 1949——.
1514. *Sowjetstudien*. Munich: Institute for the Study of the USSR. 1956——.
1515. *Sowjetwissenschaft: Gesellschaftswissenschaftliche Beiträge*. Gesellschaft für Deutsch-Sowjetische Freundschaft. Berlin: Verlag Kultur und Fortschritt. 1948——.
1516. *Unter dem Banner des Marxismus*. Vienna. 1925–35.
1517. *Vorwärts: Zentral-Organ der Sozialdemokratie Deutschlands*. Leipzig. 1876–78.

1518. *Critica Marxista*. Rome, Italy. 1963——.

38 ———————— BIBLIOGRAPHIES AND REFERENCE WORKS

The beginner might find 1529 and 1534 of considerable value. Both provide elementary explanations of the central terms of Marxist theory and practice. 1551, 1556, and 1557 concentrate on the work of the classics of Marxism. 1525 is a good introductory guide in English. Hunt's 1533 is a selected, annotated bibliography on the theory and practice of Communism. Unfortunately, it lists only a relatively small number of philosophical works. 1535 is somewhat more complete than Hunt's book; 1524 is virtually exhaustive, but covers only a short period. 1536 is an excellent list of works. Its major shortcoming is that it was compiled without philosophical sophistication—occasionally even without a grasp of the books reviewed. 1539 is a much shorter list and contains little of philosophical interest.

1523 and 1530 are useful works; their value for the study of dialectical and historical materialism, however, is minimal. 1540 is an interesting, though miscellaneous, list. 1526 is a book of great potential usefulness; unfortunately, however, Delaney's comments render it valueless. He takes great pains to distinguish between those who are on "the right side" and those who are not, and writes as if no more were needed to destroy a book than to call it "liberal" or, worse yet, "secular." 1519 is a valuable bibliographical yearbook for students of Soviet philosophy and intellectual life. 1531 is a remarkable annotated bibliography of 7,000 books in 30 languages; some of the books have considerable philosophical relevance. 1532 is a useful guide to Western language publications about Russia and the Soviet Union.

1520 carries bibliographies on all aspects—practical as well as theoretical—of Marxism-Leninism. 1537 contains a good bibliography of the works of Marx and of works critical of him. 1550 is a short bibliography of Marx. Rubel's 1545, on the other hand, is an important, major effort; it is certainly the best bibliography we have of Marx's works. 1542 indexes and annotates articles appearing in over forty Marxist journals. 1548 is an equally thorough international bibliography of the journal literature of Marxism. 1538, 1541, 1543, 1544, and 1546 are general bibliographies of philosophy. Although they do not contain special lists of Marxist-Leninist works, such books are regularly reviewed in them. The reader will find these general bibliographies of use in keeping up with new publications on Marxist philosophy. They are also of value in providing the scholar with some pointers concerning the relevance of a given book to his field of research. 1547 is a bibliography of the works of the Soviet philosopher Deborin; 1552 details the works of the dialectical materialist Nikolai Bukharin.

1519. The American Bibliography of Russian and East European Studies. Bloomington, Ind.: Indiana University Publications, 1956——.

1520. THE AMERICAN INSTITUTE FOR MARXIST STUDIES. Newsletter. 1964——.

1521. APTHEKER, HERBERT. A Bibliography on Marxism and Democracy. New York: American Institute for Marxist Studies, 1966.

1522. Bibliography of the Writings of Leon Trotsky Published in English Press and Bulletins. N.p., 1959. 1 vol., unpaged.

1523. Bibliography on the Communist Problem in the United States. New York: Fund for the Republic, 1955. 474p.

1524. Books on Communism (1950–1956): A Reader's Guide (no author). London?: 1956? 148p.

1525. CORNFORTH, MAURICE C. Reader's Guide to the Marxist Classics. London: Lawrence & Wishart, 1952. 114p.

1526. DELANEY, ROBERT F. The Literature of Communism in America: A Selected Reference Guide. Washington, D.C.: Catholic University of America Press, 1962. 433p.

1527. DOSSICK, JESSE J., ed. Doctoral Research on Russia and the Soviet Union. New York: New York University Press, 1960. 248p.

1528. FOLSOM, MICHAEL B. Shakespeare: A Marxist Bibliography. New York: American Institute for Marxist Studies, 1965. 9p.

1529. GOULD, L. HARRY. Marxist Glossary. Sydney: Current Book Distributors, 1946. 99p.

1530. GRIERSON, PHILIP. Books on Soviet Russia, 1917–1942. London: Methuen, 1943. 354p.

1531. HAMMOND, THOMAS T., ed. Soviet Foreign Relations and World Communism. Princeton: Princeton University Press, 1965. 1240p.

1532. HORECKY, PAUL L., ed. Russia and the Soviet Union. Chicago: University of Chicago Press, 1965. 473p.

1533. HUNT, ROBERT N. C. Books on Communism. London: Ampersand Ltd., 1959. 333p.

1534. ———. A Guide to Communist Jargon. New York: Macmillan, 1957. 169p.

1535. KOLARZ, W., ed. Books on Communism. New York: Oxford University Press, 1964. 568p.

1536. MARX, KARL. Capital. London & Toronto: Dent, 1930. 2 vols.

1537. *Philosophical Books: A Quarterly Review*. Leicester, Eng.: Leicester University Press, 1960——.

1538. UNITED STATES LIBRARY OF CONGRESS. Legislative Reference Service. *World Communism; A Selected Annotated Bibliography*. Harrisburg: Department of Public Instruction, Commonwealth of Pennsylvania, 1958. 20p.

1539. UNITED STATES LIBRARY OF CONGRESS. Legislative Reference Service. *World Communism: A Selected Annotated Bibliography*. Washington, D.C.: Government Printing Office, 1964. 394p.

1540. WILCOX, THOMAS. *The Anti-Bolshevik Bibliography*. Los Angeles: Privately printed, 1954. 76p.

1541. *Bibliographie de la Philosophie*. Paris: Institut International de Philosophie. 1954——.

1542. *Bibliographie marxiste international*. Paris: Centre d'Études et de Recherches Marxistes. 1964——.

1543. DE BRIE, G. A., ed. *Bibliographia philosophica*. Utrecht. 1934–45.

1544. FRANCE. CENTRE NATIONAL DE LA RECHERCHE SCIENTIFIQUE. *Bulletin analytique: Philosophie*. 1947——.

1545. RUBEL, MAXIMILIEN. *Bibliographie des oeuvres de Karl Marx; avec en appendice un répertoire des oeuvres de Friedrich Engels*. Paris: M. Rivière, 1956. 272p. Supplément. Paris. 1960.

1546. SOCIETÉ FRANÇAISE DE PHILOSOPHIE. *Bulletin*. Paris. 1901——.

1547. AHLBERG, RENÉ. *A. M. Deborin*. Berlin: In Kommission bei Otto Harrassowitz, 1959. 27p.

1548. BERLIN. INSTITUT FÜR MARXISMUS-LENINISMUS. *Internationale Bibliographie der marxistischen Zeitschriftenliteratur*. Berlin: Dietz, Juli/Dez. 1950——.

1549. *Das Literarische Werk der Klassiker des Marxismus-Leninismus. Ein erläuternder Auswahlverzeichnis*. Berlin: Magistrat von Gross-Berlin, 1953. 132p.

1550. GERMANY (DEMOCRATIC REPUBLIC). ZENTRALINSTITUT FÜR BIBLIOTHEKSWESEN. *Karl Marx, eine empfehlende Bibliographie*. Prepared by Rittner, Werner. Leipzig: Verlag für Buch- und Bibliothekswesen, 1954. 54p.

1551. GOLLWITZER, HELMUT, und LEHMBRUCH, GERHARD. *Kleiner Wegweiser zum Studium des Marxismus-Leninismus*. Bonn: Publikationsstelle des Bundesministeriums für Gesamtdeutsche Fragen, 1956. 23p.

1552. HEITMAN, SIDNEY, und KNIRSCH, PETER. *N. I. Bucharin.* Berlin: In Kommission bei Otto Harrassowitz, 1959. 93p.

1553. LEHMBRUCH, GERHARD. *Kleiner Wegweiser zum Studium der Sowjetideologie.* Bonn: Publikationsstelle des Bundesministeriums für Gesamtdeutsche Fragen, 1958. 90p.

1554. LEVIN, LEO A. *Die Klassiker des Marxismus-Leninismus in empfehlenden Bibliographien.* Leipzig: O. Harrassowitz, 1953. 36p.

1555. MÜHEPFORDT, GÜNTER. "Marx und Russland," Eine Bibliographie von Veröffentlichungen, unveröffentlichten Arbeiten und Fotokopien aus der UdSSR, der Volksrepublik Polen und der DDR (1945–59), in *Jahrbuch für Geschichte der UdSSR und der Volksdemokratischen Länder Europas.* Band 3. Berlin: Rütten und Loening, 1959, 489–95.

1556. *Verzeichnis der wichtigsten Literatur für das Studium des Grundlagen des Marxismus-Leninismus.* Berlin: Dietz, 1952. 20p.

1557. *Werke und Schriften des wissenschaftlichen Sozialismus.* Leipzig: Leipziger Kommissions und Grossbuchhandlung, 1955. 124p.

See also: 122, 152, 249, 296, 302, 1188, 1217, 1225, 1257, 1271, 1490.

INDEX

(References are to page numbers)